FAMILY
MEALS

366

RECIPES

FAMILY
MEALS

SUNBURST BOOKS

CONTENTS

SOUPS

COUNTRY SOUP
Serves 4–6

1 oz (25 g) butter
3 medium onions, finely chopped
1 lb (450 g) white cabbage, cored and shredded
3 large cooking apples, peeled, cored and chopped
2 pt (1.2 L) chicken stock
1 tsp brown sugar
salt and freshly ground black pepper
4 rashers streaky bacon
4 tbsp double cream

Melt the butter in a large, heavy pan and sauté the onions for about 5 minutes until pale golden in colour. Add the cabbage and apples, cover the pan and sweat for a further 5 minutes. Add the stock and sugar, bring to the boil, cover with a tight fitting lid and simmer gently on a low heat for about 1 hour. A little more stock or water may be added halfway through the cooking time if needed. Remove half of the soup and purée in a blender, then return to the pan and simmer for a further 30 minutes. Fry or grill the bacon rashers, chop up and sprinkle an equal amount into each soup bowl. Stir in the cream before serving.

CREAM OF MUSHROOM SOUP
Serves 4

2 oz (50 g) butter
8 oz (225 g) mushrooms, finely chopped
1 small onion or 3 spring onions, finely chopped
2 oz (50 g) plain flour
1 pt (600 ml) vegetable or chicken stock
¾ pt (450 ml) milk
salt and freshly ground black pepper

Melt the butter in a saucepan and fry the mushrooms and onion for 5 minutes, stirring constantly. Gradually stir in the flour and cook for 3 minutes. Remove from the heat and pour in the stock a little at a time, followed by the milk. Blend thoroughly, return to the heat and bring to the boil. Cook until the soup thickens. Add salt and pepper to taste.

LETTUCE SOUP
Serves 4

2 oz (50 g) butter
12 oz (350 g) lettuce leaves, chopped
4 oz (110 g) spring onions, trimmed and chopped
1 tbsp plain flour
1 pt (600 ml) chicken stock
¼ pt (150 ml) milk
salt and freshly ground black pepper

Heat the butter in a deep saucepan and cook the lettuce and spring onions until soft. Gradually stir in the flour and pour in the stock. Bring to the boil, cover, lower the heat and simmer for 15–20 minutes. Remove from the heat and leave to cool. Pour into a blender and purée, then return to the saucepan. Pour in the milk and salt and pepper to taste and reheat until hot enough to serve.

CREAMY VEGETABLE SOUP
Serves 4

1 oz (25 g) butter
1 lb (450 g) carrots, diced
1 medium onion, chopped
2 medium potatoes, diced
½ small swede, diced
1 small red pepper, deseeded and chopped
¾ pt (450 ml) water or vegetable stock
2 oz (50 g) lentils
salt and freshly ground black pepper
1 bay leaf
1½ oz (35 g) plain flour
¾ pt (450 ml) milk
4 oz (110 g) Cheddar cheese, grated
croûtons to garnish

Melt the butter in a saucepan, add the carrots, onion, potatoes, swede and pepper and sauté until soft. Add the water or stock, lentils, salt, pepper and bay leaf and simmer for 30 minutes. Mix the flour with a little of the milk and then blend in the remaining milk. Stir into the soup until it thickens. Simmer for 5 minutes and then stir in the cheese. Serve with crisp fried croûtons.

FLOATING ISLAND SOUP
Serves 4

1 small onion, finely chopped
2 oz (50 g) butter
1 oz (25 g) plain flour
1 pt (600 ml) milk
salt and freshly ground black pepper
4 oz (110 g) Cheddar cheese, grated
2 eggs, separated
2 tbsp chopped fresh parsley

Sauté the onion in the butter for a few minutes until soft but not browned. Stir in the flour and cook for about 1 minute, stirring. Add the milk gradually and stir until boiling. Season well and simmer gently for another 5 minutes. Mix in the cheese, 1 tablespoon of the parsley and the beaten egg yolks. Reheat very gently until the cheese has melted without allowing it to boil. Whisk the egg whites until stiff and put teaspoonfuls into the soup bowls, pouring the hot soup over them. Sprinkle with the remaining chopped parsley.

MINESTRONE SOUP
Serves 6–8

8 oz (225 g) broad beans
3 sticks celery, chopped
1 onion, sliced
2 garlic cloves, crushed
8 oz (225 g) tomatoes, peeled and quartered
2 carrots, diced
4 oz (110 g) brown rice
2 tbsp chopped fresh parsley or a small bunch tied with thick thread
3 pt (1.8 L) beef stock
salt and freshly ground black pepper
8 oz (225 g) spinach, finely chopped
Parmesan cheese
1 tbsp chopped parsley

Place all the ingredients, except the spinach, Parmesan cheese and parsley, in a very large saucepan and bring to the boil. Reduce the heat, cover and simmer gently for 30 minutes, then add the spinach and continue to simmer until all the vegetables are tender. Add more seasoning if required, then pour into serving bowls and sprinkle with Parmesan cheese and parsley.

CREAM OF APPLE SOUP
Serves 4

1 oz (25 g) butter
1 oz (25 g) plain flour
1 pt (600 ml) milk
1½ lb (675 g) apples, peeled, cored and grated
sugar to taste
juice of 1 lemon
7 fl oz (200 ml) dry cider

Make a white sauce by melting the butter in a saucepan and stirring in the flour. Let it cook for 1 minute and gradually add the milk stirring all the time. Simmer for about 5 minutes, whisking from time to time to avoid lumps forming. Set aside and keep warm. Simmer the apples until soft, with just enough water to prevent burning, sugar to taste and add the lemon juice. Sieve into the hot sauce and stir in the cider. Whisk well and serve.

SPINACH SOUP
Serves 6

2 oz (50 g) butter
6 oz (175 g) packet frozen spinach, thawed and chopped
1 onion, finely chopped
1 oz (25 g) plain flour
½ pt (300 ml) chicken stock
1 pt (600 ml) milk
pinch grated nutmeg
salt and freshly ground black pepper
2 tbsp single cream

Melt the butter in a large saucepan and cook the spinach and onions gently for 5 minutes. Stir in the flour gradually. Remove from the heat. Pour in the stock, return to the heat and boil, stirring constantly until the soup thickens. Carefully pour in the milk, blending well and bring back to the boil, stirring. Lower the heat, cover and simmer for 15–20 minutes. Add the nutmeg and seasoning to taste. Remove from the heat, leave to cool slightly and purée in a blender or by passing through a sieve. Add a little milk to thin the soup if necessary. Return to the saucepan and reheat. Just before serving, stir in the cream.

CREAM OF TOMATO SOUP
Serves 4

1oz (25 g) margarine or butter
1 tbsp sunflower oil
1 large onion, finely chopped
2 oz (50 g) plain flour
1 pt (600 ml) water
½ pt (300 ml) milk
14 oz (400 g) can tomatoes
5 oz (150 g) can tomato purée
2 tsp light Muscavado sugar
salt and freshly ground black pepper

Heat the fat and oil in a saucepan and fry the onion until golden brown. Gradually stir in the flour and cook for 1 minute. Pour in the water and milk and bring to the boil. Stir constantly until the soup thickens slightly. Mix in the tomatoes, purée and sugar, and season to taste with salt and pepper. Cook over low heat for 20 minutes until the onion is tender. Sieve or liquidise then reheat and taste for seasoning before serving.

CHINESE MIMOSA SOUP
Serves 6–8

1½ lb (675 g) onions, finely chopped
2 oz (50 g) butter
1 oz (25 g) plain flour
2 pt (1.2 L) chicken or vegetable stock
8 button mushrooms, sliced
salt and freshly ground black pepper
3 oz (75 g) Edam cheese
fresh parsley, finely chopped

Sweat the onions without browning for about 5 minutes in the melted butter. Stir in the flour and cook for a further minute, then add the hot stock gradually. Bring to the boil and then reduce the heat and simmer for at least 30 minutes or until the onion is thoroughly cooked and soft. Stir in the finely sliced button mushrooms and season to taste. Simmer for about 4 minutes. Ladle the soup into soup bowls, grate the cheese through a coarse grater on top of the soup and sprinkle with parsley.

CHICKEN SOUP WITH CHEESE DUMPLINGS
Serves 4

1 small boiling fowl or chicken, with giblets
1 onion, chopped
1 carrot, diced
1 leek, diced
1 bay leaf
fresh parsley and thyme sprigs
salt and freshly ground black pepper
2½ pt (1.4 L) water

Dumplings:
4 oz (110 g) quark or curd cheese
1 beaten egg
1 tbsp butter, melted
7 oz (200 g) plain flour
2 tbsp chopped fresh parsley

Put the bird in a large saucepan with all the vegetables and herbs, and season to taste. Pour in the water and bring to the boil. Cover and simmer for about 2 hours or until the meat is tender. Remove the chicken to use for another meal. Continue to boil the soup until the liquid has reduced by about one-third. To make the dumplings, put the quark, egg and butter in a bowl and mix to a smooth paste. Beat in the flour, a pinch of salt and the parsley. Knead into a dough and, using floured hands, form into small balls. Drop these into the soup and cook for 8–10 minutes.

CHICKEN NOODLE SOUP
Serves 4

1½ pt (900 ml) chicken stock
2 oz (50 g) vermicelli, broken up
4 spring onions, sliced
salt and freshly ground black pepper
2 oz (50 g) cooked chicken, chopped
1 tbsp chopped fresh parsley

Bring the stock to the boil. Add the vermicelli, stirring well until stock returns to the boil. Add the onions and season to taste with salt and pepper. Lower the heat and cook for 6–8 minutes until the vermicelli is cooked. Mix in the chicken and parsley and reheat to serve.

PEA SOUP
Serves 4

2 oz (50 g) butter
1 small onion, finely chopped
2 lb (900 g) fresh peas, shelled
½ tsp caster sugar
2 large mint sprigs
2 pt (1.2 L) chicken stock
salt and freshly ground black pepper
2 egg yolks
¼ pt (150 ml) double cream

Melt the butter in a saucepan, and fry the onion for 5 minutes until soft, but not brown. Add the peas, sugar, mint and stock. Bring to the boil, lower the heat and cook for 30 minutes. Purée the soup in a blender or pass through a sieve, return to the pan and add salt and freshly ground black pepper to taste. Place the egg yolks and cream in a bowl and beat thoroughly. Gradually mix into the soup and heat very gently, stirring constantly, but do not boil. Serve at once.

CHEESE SOUP
Serves 4

10½ oz (310 g) can condensed consommé
6 fl oz (180 ml) water
4 oz (110 g) Emmenthal cheese, finely grated
4 fl oz (125 ml) double cream
2 large egg yolks

Pour the consommé and water into a saucepan. Place over a low heat and gradually add the cheese, stirring constantly. Bring to just below boiling point, then remove from the heat. In a small bowl, beat together the cream and egg yolks, then stir into the soup using a wooden spoon. Return to a low heat and cook, stirring constantly, until the soup thickens. Do not allow the mixture to boil or it will curdle.

BEEF TEA
Serves 6

2 lb (900 g) shin beef, trimmed and cubed
1 small onion, very finely chopped
1 carrot, very finely chopped
2 pt (1.2 L) boiling water
1 bay leaf
dash of soy sauce
freshly ground black pepper

Heat the oven to 300°F/150°C/Gas Mk 2. Bring all the ingredients to the boil in an ovenproof casserole and cover with a very tight lid. A piece of foil may be placed over the casserole first to give a really tight fit. Simmer for 3–4 hours or until the meat is very tender. Strain into a large bowl and leave to cool. When ready to serve, skim off any fat and reheat gently in a saucepan. A teaspoon of Marmite or similar meat extract may be added to give colour. Serve with thin hot toast.

WHITE BEAN SOUP WITH SMOKED SAUSAGE
Serves 4

1 tbsp oil
2 onions, chopped
1 tbsp plain flour
4 oz (110 g) haricot beans, soaked overnight and drained
1 pt (600 ml) chicken stock
14 oz (400 g) can chopped tomatoes
8 oz (225 g) piece German salami or schinkenwurst, skinned
½ tsp dried thyme
salt and freshly ground black pepper

Heat the oil in a saucepan and cook the onions until slightly brown. Stir in the flour, followed by the beans. Pour in the stock, stirring constantly, and bring to the boil. Simmer for 2–3 minutes. Add the tomatoes, sausage, thyme and seasoning to taste. Cover and simmer for 1½ hours or until the beans are soft. Remove the sausage, slice thinly and then return to the soup.

ONION SOUP
Serves 4

3 tbsp oil
1 lb (450 g) onions, thinly sliced
2 tbsp plain flour
3½ pt (2 L) vegetable stock
salt and freshly ground black pepper
8 oz (225 g) sliced bread
4 oz (110 g) Cheddar cheese, grated

Heat the oil in a large saucepan and sauté the onions until just turning golden. Stir in the flour, add the stock and cook over a low heat for 10 minutes. Season to taste with salt and pepper. Meanwhile, toast the bread slices. Pour the soup into an ovenproof dish, top with the pieces of toasted bread and the grated cheese. Bake in the oven at 425°F/220°C/Gas Mk 7 for 5–10 minutes or reheat the soup and brown the topping under the grill.

GOULASH SOUP
Serves 8

2 oz (50 g) lard or 3 tbsp oil
1 lb (450 g) stewing steak, trimmed and finely diced
1 lb (450 g) onions, finely chopped
1 tbsp paprika
14 oz (400 g) can chopped tomatoes
2 beef stock cubes, chopped
1¾ pt (1 L) water
1 lb (450 g) potatoes, diced
2 green peppers, deseeded and chopped
salt and freshly ground black pepper

Heat the lard or oil in a large saucepan, and cook the steak and onions, stirring, until lightly brown. Add the paprika, tomatoes, stock cubes and water and stir well. Bring to the boil, stirring constantly, then cover and simmer for 1 hour. Add the potatoes and green peppers. Cover and simmer for 30 minutes, then season to taste.

SPINACH AND OATMEAL SOUP
Serves 4

2 tbsp olive oil
2 onions, sliced
2 lb (900 g) spinach, cooked and drained
4 tbsp oatmeal
1¾ pt (1 L) water
7 fl oz (200 ml) milk
1 tsp soya sauce
salt

Heat the oil in a saucepan and sauté the onions until soft. Add the spinach, oatmeal and water then cover and cook for 20 minutes. Stir in the milk, then purée the mixture in a blender or pass through a sieve. Reheat the soup, season with the soya sauce and salt and serve immediately.

BEAN AND BACON SOUP
Serves 4

6 oz (175 g) haricot beans
4 rashers smoked back bacon, derinded and chopped
1 medium onion, chopped
1 small garlic clove, crushed
1 tbsp oil
½ tsp dried rosemary
2½ pt (1.4 L) chicken stock
2 oz (50 g) Red Leicester cheese, grated
salt and freshly ground black pepper
croûtons, to garnish

Place the beans in a large bowl and cover with boiling water. Leave for 3 hours, then drain. Gently sauté the chopped bacon, onion and garlic in a saucepan in a little oil for about 5 minutes or until beginning to soften. Add the beans, rosemary and stock, bring to the boil and simmer gently for about 1 hour or until the beans are tender. Remove as many pieces of bacon as possible, together with about half the beans and set aside. Purée the remainder of the soup in a blender or pass through a sieve. Return to a clean pan, add the cheese, bacon and remaining beans, adjust the seasoning and reheat gently. Serve with crisply fried bread croûtons.

SAUSAGE AND POTATO CHOWDER
Serves 6

1 oz (25 g) butter
2 large onions, sliced
4 large leeks, trimmed and sliced
¼ tsp caraway seeds
2 lb (900 g) potatoes, diced
2½ pt (1.4 L) chicken stock
salt and freshly ground black pepper
8 oz (225 g) German sausage, diced
4 tbsp soured cream
¼ tsp nutmeg

Melt the butter in a saucepan, and cook the onions, leeks and caraway seeds for 3–4 minutes. Add the potatoes and stock and season to taste. Bring to the boil, then simmer for 45 minutes. Add the sausage, cream and nutmeg, stir well and reheat gently.

LEEK SOUP
Serves 4

1 lb (450 g) leeks, trimmed and sliced
1 lb (450 g) potatoes, peeled and chopped
vegetable stock or water
¾ pt (450 ml) hot milk
1 oz (25 g) butter
salt and freshly ground black pepper

Place the leeks and potatoes in a large saucepan with enough cold water or vegetable stock to cover. Simmer, covered, for about 30 minutes. Purée the mixture in a blender or pass through a sieve, then return to the pan. Add the hot milk and continue to cook for a further 5 minutes, stirring constantly. Stir in the butter and seasoning to taste, and serve.

GENOESE VEGETABLE SOUP
Serves 4

3 oz (75 g) peas
1 lb (450 g) potatoes, peeled and cubed
2 bunches watercress, trimmed and chopped
1 leek, trimmed and sliced
1 aubergine, cubed
1 celery stick, sliced
2 tomatoes, peeled and chopped
2 pt (1.2 L) water or stock

Paste:
1 tbsp chopped fresh basil
1 tbsp chopped fresh parsley
1 tbsp olive oil
150 g (5 oz) pasta shells
salt and freshly ground black pepper
2 oz (50 g) grated Parmesan cheese

Place all the vegetables in a saucepan with the water or stock. Bring to
the boil, cover and simmer for 20 minutes until just tender.
Meanwhile, using a pestle and mortar or a food processor, blend the
herbs and olive oil to a paste. Add the pasta shells and herb paste to
the vegetables and continue cooking for 10 minutes or until the pasta
is cooked. Season well and serve sprinkled with the Parmesan cheese.

FISH

NORMANDY COD
Serves 4

4 cod steaks
2 cooking apples, peeled and cored
knob of butter
1 tbsp tomato purée
2½ tbsp quick porridge oats
½ tsp salt
1 tsp sugar

Preheat the oven to 350°F/180°C/Gas Mk 4. Gently simmer the cooking apples with a little butter and water until mushy. Strain off any extra juice leaving a firm purée. Mix in the tomato purée, oats, salt and sugar and cook for 1 minute. Put the fish into a buttered shallow ovenproof dish and cover with the apple mixture. Bake in a preheated oven for 30–40 minutes. Garnish with lemon.

SOMERSET FISH
Serves 4

4 trout or herring
salt and freshly ground black pepper
3 small onions, sliced into rings
2 dessert apples, peeled, cored and finely chopped
pinch cinnamon
juice of 2 oranges
¼ pt (150 ml) fish stock
2 bay leaves
orange slices, to garnish

Preheat the oven to 375°F/190°C/Gas Mk 5. Thoroughly wash and dry the fish and sprinkle with salt and pepper to taste. Place in a casserole dish. Add the onions, apples and cinnamon, orange juice and fish stock. Add the bay leaves and cook in the oven for 30–35 minutes. Garnish with the orange slices and serve at once.

PLAICE FLORENTINE
Serves 4

4 large fillets of plaice, skinned
salt and freshly ground black pepper
juice of ½ lemon
2 oz (50 g) margarine
2 oz (50 g) plain flour
1 pt (600 ml) milk
1½ lb (675 g) fresh spinach, cooked and drained
2 oz (50 g) Cheddar cheese, grated
1 oz (25 g) brown breadcrumbs

Preheat the oven to 400°F/200°C/Gas Mk 6. Sprinkle salt and pepper
and the lemon juice on the fillets and roll them up. Heat the
margarine in a saucepan, stir in the flour and cook for 1 minute.
Gradually pour in the milk and bring to the boil, stirring constantly
until thickened. Add salt and pepper to taste. Mix about ¼ pt (150 ml)
of the sauce with the spinach and place in a 2 pt (1.2 L) ovenproof
dish. Arrange the rolled fillets on top of the spinach and pour over the
remaining sauce. Mix the cheese and breadcrumbs together and
sprinkle over the top. Bake in the oven for 20 minutes until the top is
golden brown.

TUNA SOUFFLÉ
Serves 4

3½ oz (85 g) can tuna
1 oz (25 g) butter
1 oz (25 g) plain flour
½ pt (300 ml) milk
3 egg yolks
salt and freshly ground black pepper
4 egg whites

Preheat the oven to 375°F/190°C/Gas Mk 5. Mash the tuna. Melt the
butter in a saucepan and stir in the flour. Cook for about 1 minute
and then add the milk, still stirring, and cook for a further minute.
Remove from the heat and stir in the three egg yolks, one at a time,
then the tuna and season well. Whisk the egg whites until stiff and
fold into the tuna sauce. Pour into a well buttered 6 inch (15 cm)
soufflé dish and bake in the centre of the oven for 30 minutes or until
well risen and golden brown on top. Serve immediately.

HEDGERLEY COD
Serves 4

6 oz (175 g) brown rice
4 cod cutlets
1½ oz (35 g) margarine
1 oz (25 g) plain flour
½ pt (300 ml) milk
freshly ground black pepper
8 oz (225 g) tomatoes
4 oz (110 g) Cheddar cheese, grated

Preheat the oven to 400°F/200°C/Gas Mk 6. Cook the rice as directed on the packet. Lightly grease a large, shallow ovenproof dish and pile the cooked and drained rice around the outside. Place the cod cutlets in the middle. Melt the margarine in a saucepan, stir in the flour and cook for 1 minute. Gradually pour in the milk and bring to the boil, stirring constantly, until thickened. Add pepper to taste, then pour the sauce over the cod cutlets. Slice the tomatoes and arrange on top of the rice. Sprinkle the cheese over the top and bake in the oven for 30 minutes until the fish is tender and the cheese has browned.

COD WITH ORANGE AND WALNUTS
Serves 4

2 oz (50 g) butter
3 oz (75 g) fresh breadcrumbs
1 garlic clove, finely chopped
1 oz (25 g) walnuts, finely chopped
finely grated rind and juice of 1 orange
4 cod cutlets
salt and freshly ground black pepper

Preheat the oven to 375°F/190°C/Gas Mk 5. Melt the butter in a saucepan, and stir in the breadcrumbs, garlic, walnuts and orange rind. Simmer over low heat, stirring from time to time, until the breadcrumbs have absorbed the butter. Arrange the cod in a buttered ovenproof dish and season to taste with salt and pepper. Pour over the orange juice, then cover with the breadcrumb mixture. Bake in the oven for 20–30 minutes until the fish is tender.

COD PORTUGAISE
Serves 4

1 tbsp oil
1 medium onion, finely chopped
1 green pepper, deseeded and finely sliced
4 medium tomatoes, peeled
1 lb (450 g) cod fillets
1 tbsp plain flour
salt and freshly ground black pepper
1–2 tbsp oil
2 oz (50 g) butter
6 fl oz (180 ml) white wine
12 stuffed olives, sliced (optional)

Heat the oil in a saucepan and sauté the chopped onion gently until soft but not coloured. Add the sliced pepper and continue cooking gently. Skin the tomatoes, quarter them, remove the seeds and chop the flesh. Add to the onion mixture and keep warm. Skin the cod fillets, cut into four pieces and coat with seasoned flour. Heat the remaining oil together with the butter in a large frying pan and fry the fish briskly until the underside is browned. Carefully turn over and cook the other side until golden brown. Add the wine and olives (if using) to the onion mixture and heat. Pour some of the sauce into a heated serving dish and place the cod on top. Serve the remaining sauce separately.

BAKED TURBOT WITH YOGHURT
Serves 4

1 lb (450 g) turbot
½ pt (300 ml) yoghurt
1 tbsp lemon juice
1 tbsp dry sherry
1 blade of mace
1 egg yolk
salt and freshly ground black pepper

Preheat the oven to 375°F/190°C/Gas Mk 5. Thoroughly clean the turbot and arrange in an ovenproof dish. Put the yoghurt, lemon juice, sherry, mace and egg yolk in a bowl and beat well. Season to taste with salt and pepper. Pour over the turbot, cover with foil and bake in the oven for 45–50 minutes.

TOMATO SPICED COD STEAKS
Serves 4

1 oz (25 g) fresh parsley, finely chopped
1 small onion, finely chopped
2 small bacon rashers, derinded and chopped
1 oz (25 g) butter
4 cod steaks
juice of 1 lemon
2 peppercorns
2 cloves

Tomato sauce:
1 oz (25 g) butter
1 small onion, diced
1 bacon rasher, derinded and chopped
14 oz (400 g) can tomatoes
1 bay leaf
2 oz (50 g) plain flour
¼ pt (150 ml) stock
good pinch sugar
salt and freshly ground black pepper

Preheat the oven to 425°F/220°C/Gas Mk 7. Mix together the parsley, onion and bacon. Butter a shallow ovenproof dish and arrange the fish in it. Spread some butter over the cod steaks, squeeze over the lemon juice and add a scattering of salt. Sprinkle the top with the onion, bacon and parsley mixture and bake in the oven for 20 minutes or until the fish is cooked. To make the tomato sauce, heat the butter in a small saucepan and toss the onion and bacon until soft but not browned. Add the tomatoes and bay leaf and simmer for a few minutes until soft. Blend the flour with the stock, add to the tomato mixture and simmer for about 30 minutes. Add the sugar and seasoning, remove the bay leaf and blend to a purée. Add the peppercorns and cloves. Gently reheat the tomato sauce and serve separately.

FISH CROQUETTES
Serves 4

12 oz (350 g) white fish
4 oz (110 g) potatoes, cooked and mashed
salt and freshly ground black pepper
tomato ketchup
chopped fresh parsley
1 egg, beaten
dry breadcrumbs
oil for frying

Steam the fish and flake the flesh, removing any bones and skin. Mix together the potatoes and fish and season to taste with salt and pepper. Stir in 1 tbsp tomato ketchup and parsley to taste. Mix together thoroughly and shape into small croquettes between floured hands. Roll in seasoned flour, then in the egg and finally in the breadcrumbs. Chill in the refrigerator for 30 minutes to firm up and then fry in hot oil until golden brown.

FISH PIE
Serves 4

1 oz (25 g) butter
1 oz (25 g) plain flour
½ pt (300 ml) milk
salt and freshly ground black pepper
1 lb (450 g) white fish, cooked
4 oz (110 g) peeled prawns
2 eggs, hard-boiled, shelled and roughly chopped
1 oz (25 g) butter
1 lb (450 g) potatoes, cooked and mashed

Preheat the oven to 375°F/190°C/Gas Mk 5. Make a white sauce: melt the butter, stir in the flour and cook gently for 1 minute. Then add the milk gradually and cook, stirring, for about 5 minutes. Season with salt and pepper to taste. Remove any skin and bones from the fish and flake the flesh. Mix the fish, prawns and eggs with the white sauce and pour into a buttered deep ovenproof dish. Spread the mashed potatoes over the top and brown in the oven.

COD IN GARLIC MARINADE
Serves 4

4 x 6 oz (175 g) cod cutlets
2 tsp lemon juice
salt and freshly ground black pepper
3 garlic cloves, crushed with a little salt
4–5 tbsp oil
1 oz (25 g) butter
1 tbsp chopped fresh parsley

Preheat the oven to 400°F/200°C/Gas Mk 6. Rinse and dry the cod. Sprinkle over the lemon juice and leave for 15 minutes. Sprinkle salt and pepper to taste on both sides of the cutlets. Place the garlic and oil in a bowl, mix well and dip the cutlets into this mixture until they are well coated with the marinade. Place the cutlets in an ovenproof dish and dot each with butter. Bake in the oven for 15–20 minutes, basting with the marinade from time to time. Sprinkle over the parsley and serve at once.

TUNA AND YOGHURT FLAN
Serves 4–6

3 oz (75 g) plain flour
3 oz (75 g) plain wholemeal flour
¼ tsp onion salt
2 tbsp poppy seeds
1½ oz (35 g) butter
1½ oz (35 g) lard
2 eggs
8 oz (225 g) plain Greek yoghurt
2 tbsp chopped chives
10 oz (300 g) canned tuna, drained
chopped fresh chives, to garnish

To make the pastry, sift the flours into a bowl with the onion salt, mix the poppy seeds into the dough and then rub in the fats. Mix with enough cold water to form a firm dough. Wrap in clingfilm and chill for 20 minutes. Preheat the oven to 400°F/200°C/Gas Mk 6. Line an 8 inch (20 cm) flan tin or ring with the pastry and bake blind for 15 minutes. Lower the oven heat to 375°F/190°C/Gas Mk 5. Whisk the eggs with the yoghurt and stir in the chives. Season to taste. Gently flake the tuna and stir into the yoghurt mixture. Spoon into the pastry case and bake for 30 minutes until set and golden. Serve hot or cold with a sprinkling of chopped chives on top.

STEAMED TROUT WITH MUSHROOMS
Serves 4

4 trout
¼ tsp salt
freshly ground black pepper
4 tbsp lemon juice
fresh dill sprigs
2–3 oz (50–75 g) mushrooms, sliced

Thoroughly clean the fish and arrange them on a large piece of foil.
Sprinkle with salt, pepper, lemon juice and dill. Fold over the foil
securely so that the juice does not run out. Place between two large
plates then place the plates over a saucepan of boiling water. Steam for
10–15 minutes until cooked and transfer to a hot serving dish. Pour
the cooking juice from the foil into a small saucepan and bring to the
boil. Add the mushrooms and simmer gently for 4–5 minutes. Pour
the mushrooms and juice over the trout and serve at once.

BAKED STUFFED HADDOCK
Serves 4

1 oz (25 g) butter
1 tbsp oil
2 medium onions, chopped
1½ oz (35 g) butter
4 oz (110 g) fresh breadcrumbs
3 tbsp chopped fresh parsley
grated rind and juice of 1 lemon
salt and freshly ground black pepper
1 whole haddock, boned
1 lemon, sliced

Heat the oven to 375°F/190°C/Gas Mk 5. To make the stuffing, heat
the 1 oz (25 g) butter and the oil and fry the chopped onions until
softened. Stir in the remaining butter, breadcrumbs, parsley, lemon
rind and enough lemon juice to moisten the stuffing without making
it too wet. Season well. Wipe the boned haddock and put the stuffing
into the haddock, tying round with thin string to keep the stuffing in
place. Put the fish into a well buttered shallow ovenproof dish and
cover with buttered paper. Bake in the oven for about 12 minutes for
each 1 lb (450 g) weight of fish. Serve with lemon slices.

COD PROVENÇALE
Serves 4

1 oz (25 g) margarine
1 medium onion, chopped
4 oz (110 g) button mushrooms, sliced
14 oz (400 g) can of tomatoes
1 tsp light Muscovado sugar
salt and freshly ground black pepper
2 tbsp chopped fresh parsley
6 oz (175 g) peeled scampi tails
1 lb (450 g) fillet of cod, cut into four pieces

Preheat the oven to 375°F/190°C/Gas Mk 5. Melt the margarine in a saucepan, add the onion and fry for 5 minutes until soft. Stir in the mushrooms and the tomatoes with their juice. Bring to the boil, lower the heat and simmer until the mixture is thick and pulpy. Mix in the sugar, 1 tbsp of the parsley and salt and pepper to taste. Add the scampi tails and mix well. Pile the mixture into an ovenproof dish and arrange the four pieces of cod on top. Bake in the oven for 25 minutes until the cod is cooked. Sprinkle the remaining parsley on top and serve.

KIPPER CREAM FLAN
Serves 4

6 oz (175 g) shortcrust pastry
4 oz (110 g) cucumber, diced
2 celery sticks, chopped
4 spring onions, chopped
¼ pt (150 ml) soured cream
1 tsp lemon juice
salt and freshly ground black pepper
7 oz (200 g) can kipper fillets, drained
2 hard-boiled eggs, quartered

Prepare and bake blind an 8 inch (20 cm) flan case as in Quiche Lorraine on page 98. Return to the oven without the baking beans for 10 minutes and then leave to cool. Mix together the cucumber, celery, spring onions, soured cream and lemon juice, and season to taste with salt and pepper. Flake the kipper fillets, removing any skin or bones, and fold into the mixture. Spoon into the prepared flan case and garnish with the hard-boiled eggs and parsley. Serve cold.

MACARONI FISH PIE
Serves 4

3 oz (75 g) short cut macaroni
salt and freshly ground black pepper
1 lb (450 g) white fish
1/2 pt (300 ml) milk

Sauce:
1 oz (25 g) butter
1 oz (25 g) plain flour
½ pt (300 ml) milk
salt and freshly ground black pepper
pinch dry mustard powder
3 oz (75 g) Cheddar cheese, grated

Cook the macaroni in 2 pt (1.2 L) of boiling salted water until tender. In the meantime, place the fish in a little salted milk and simmer over a low heat until tender. Remove the fish, retaining the milk and break the fish into large flakes. To make the sauce, heat the butter in a small pan until melted. Carefully stir in the flour for 2–3 minutes. Remove from the heat and gradually pour in the milk and fish liquor and season to taste, stirring constantly. Return to the heat and bring to the boil. Boil until the sauce has thickened. Lower the heat and stir in three-quarters of the grated cheese. Arrange the fish and macaroni in a warmed serving dish and pour the cheese sauce over the top. Sprinkle the remaining cheese on top. Place under a hot grill for 3 minutes until the top is golden brown.

POULTRY AND RABBIT

CHICKEN AND BACON QUICHE
Serves 6

10 oz (300 g) shortcrust pastry, chilled for 20 minutes
2 tbsp oil
1 medium onion, sliced
8 oz (225 g) rindless back bacon, cut into small strips
15 oz (425 g) can cream of chicken soup
3 eggs
freshly ground black pepper
chopped fresh chives

Preheat the oven to 400°F/200°C/Gas Mk 6. Roll out the pastry on a lightly floured board and use it to line a 9 inch (23 cm) loose-bottomed deep flan tin. Line with foil or baking parchment filled with baking beans and bake blind for 20 minutes. Remove the parchment and beans and lower the oven heat to 375°F/190°C/Gas Mk 5. Sauté the onion in hot oil until soft, drain on kitchen paper and then place in the pastry case. Fry the bacon for a few minutes until it starts to brown, drain on kitchen paper and sprinkle over the onion. Beat the eggs with the can of chicken soup, season well with freshly ground black pepper and pour into the quiche case. Bake for 30–40 minutes in the centre of the oven. Serve hot or cold sprinkled with chopped chives.

CHICKEN AVOCADO
Serves 4

4 chicken breasts, skinned and cooked
1 large ripe avocado
1 small garlic clove, crushed
2 tbsp lemon juice
1 tbsp oil
salt and freshly ground black pepper

Cut the chicken breasts into thick slicesand arrange on a serving plate. Liquidise the avocado, garlic, lemon juice, oil and seasoning together until smooth. Spoon over the chicken dividing the sauce equally between the four chicken pieces. Serve with a crisp mixed salad and hot new potatoes.

CHICKEN AND MUSHROOM CASSEROLE
Serves 6

1 roasting chicken, cut into 6 pieces
salt and freshly ground black pepper
1½ oz (35 g) butter
2 tbsp vegetable oil
4 tbsp finely chopped onion
1 tbsp plain flour
¾ pt (450 ml) chicken stock
8 oz (225 g) mushrooms, sliced
¼ pt (150 ml) double cream
chopped fresh parsley

Preheat the oven to 350°F/180°C/Gas Mk 4. Skin the chicken pieces and pat dry. Season well with salt and freshly ground black pepper. Melt the butter and oil in a frying pan and sauté the chicken pieces until well browned, then transfer to a casserole dish. Fry the onions gently until soft and golden, then stir in the flour, mix well and pour in the chicken stock. Bring to the boil, stirring well, and simmer for 2–3 minutes. Pour the sauce over the chicken, cover the dish and cook in the centre of the oven for about 20 minutes. Scatter the sliced mushrooms over the chicken pieces, basting well with the gravy. Cook, covered, for a further 15 minutes until the chicken and mushrooms are tender. Remove the chicken and place in a warmed serving dish. Skim any fat off the top of the gravy and stir in the cream. Simmer for a minute on top of the stove and then pour over the chicken. Sprinkle with parsley.

CHICKEN PARCELS
Serves 4

2 oz (50 g) chopped bacon
2 oz (50 g) chopped mushrooms
salt and freshly ground black pepper
4 chicken quarters
a little white wine, cream or stock

Preheat the oven to 375°F/190°C/Gas Mk 5. Mix together the bacon, mushrooms and onion. Add salt and freshly ground black pepper to taste. Measure out four squares of aluminium foil and grease lightly. Place a tablespoonful of the bacon mixture on each piece of foil. Place a chicken quarter on top and pour over 1 tbsp of wine, cream or stock. Lightly close the foil to make small parcels and cook in the oven for 45 minutes, opening the foil for the last 10 minutes.

CHICKEN AND POTATO CASSEROLE
Serves 4

12 oz (350 g) small new potatoes
2 tbsp olive oil
4 chicken legs
4 oz (110 g) gammon, cut into strips
4 oz (110 g) small onions, quartered
2 garlic cloves, crushed
2 tbsp plain flour
¾ pt (450 ml) chicken stock
3 oz (75 g) button mushrooms
2 oz (50 g) green olives, stoned
1 bay leaf
1 tbsp chopped fresh parsley
salt and freshly ground black pepper

Preheat the oven to 350°F/180°C/Gas Mk 4. Place the potatoes in a saucepan of boiling salted water and parboil for about 10 minutes. Drain well. Pour the oil in a flameproof casserole, heat and add the chicken. Fry quickly, stirring, until sealed on all sides. Remove from the casserole. Place the gammon and onions in the casserole and cook until golden. Add the garlic and flour and gradually pour in the stock, stirring constantly. Cook for 2 minutes until thick. Return the chicken to the casserole together with the potatoes, mushrooms, olives and bay leaf and season with salt and pepper to taste. Bring to the boil, then lower the heat, cover and cook in the oven for 30–40 minutes until chicken is tender. To serve, sprinkle with parsley.

CHICKEN PORTUGAISE
Serves 4

4 chicken quarters
1–2 tbsp oil
salt and freshly ground black pepper
1 medium onion, sliced
4 large tomatoes, peeled and sliced
1½ oz (35 g) grated cheese

Preheat the oven to 375°F/190°C/Gas Mk 5. Brush the chicken with oil, season with salt and pepper to taste and place in a casserole dish. Place the onion on top of the chicken followed by the tomatoes and sprinkle with the cheese. Cover and cook in the oven for 50 minutes until chicken is tender. Remove the cover for the last 10 minutes of cooking time to brown the cheese.

CHICKEN BOILED WITH BEANS
Serves 6

3½ lb (1.6 kg) boiling chicken
4 oz (110 g) haricot beans, soaked overnight and drained
3 pt (1.8 L) chicken stock
2 onions, quartered
2 garlic cloves, crushed
1 bay leaf
1 tbsp dried tarragon
8 oz (225 g) can tomatoes
salt and freshly ground black pepper

Place the chicken and beans in a large saucepan with the stock. Bring to the boil, skim off the fat, then add the remaining ingredients with salt and freshly ground black pepper to taste. Cover with a lid and simmer for 2 hours or until the chicken is tender. Remove the chicken, place on a serving dish and leave to stand for 10 minutes before carving. Remove the bay leaf and press the bean mixture through a sieve to form a smooth sauce. Taste to check seasoning. Carve the chicken and serve with the bean sauce.

CHICKEN WITH GREEN PEPPERS
Serves 6

6 chicken portions
3 oz (75 g) butter
1 tbsp oil
2 onions, sliced
2 green peppers, deseeded and cut into strips
1 lb (450 g) tomatoes, peeled
1 tbsp tomato purée
salt and freshly ground black pepper
1 tsp caster sugar
1 tbsp cornflour
¼ pt (150 ml) dry white wine

Preheat the oven to 375°F/190°C/Gas Mk 5. Fry the chicken portions in the oil and butter until evenly browned all over. Remove from the pan and place in a casserole. Add the onions and peppers and sauté gently for 5 minutes until soft but not brown. Add the tomatoes, tomato purée, seasoning and sugar, stir well and simmer for another 5 minutes. Blend the cornflour with the wine and stir into the sauce. Bring to the boil and simmer for a further 2 minutes. Pour over the chicken, cover and cook in the oven for 40 minutes.

CHICKEN À LA CRÈME
Serves 4–6

1 large chicken, cut into 8 pieces
margarine, butter or oil, for frying
bouquet garni
2 rashers streaky bacon, diced
2 oz (50 g) mushrooms, sliced
1 clove garlic, crushed
½ tsp dried or several sprigs of fresh tarragon
½ pt (300 ml) dry white wine
2 egg yolks, beaten together with a little cream

Heat the fat in a large pan and cook the chicken pieces on all sides in the melted fat until sealed but not brown. Add the bouquet garni, bacon, mushrooms, garlic and tarragon. Pour in the wine, put the lid on the pan and cook very gently for about 30 minutes or until the chicken is well cooked through and tender. Remove the chicken from the pan and keep hot. Remove the bouquet garni from the pan and add the egg yolk and cream mixture. Do not let the sauce boil or it will curdle. Cook gently for 1 minute and season to taste. Pour the sauce over the chicken and serve.

CHICKEN BRAN CRUNCHY
Serves 4

4 chicken quarters
seasoned flour for coating
1 egg
4 tsp Dijon mustard
3 oz (75 g) bran flakes
3 tbsp grated Cheddar cheese
a little vegetable oil

Preheat the oven to 375°F/190°C/Gas Mk 5. Skin the chicken quarters and toss in seasoned flour. In a bowl, beat together the egg and mustard. Crush the bran flakes and mix with the cheese. Place on a flat dish and dip the chicken quarters into the egg mixture, then roll in the bran flake mixture, pressing the flakes firmly onto the chicken. Leave to stand for 5 minutes, then arrange chicken pieces in an ovenproof dish and drizzle over a little vegetable oil. Cook in the oven for 1 hour until tender. Drain on absorbent kitchen paper and serve at once.

CHICKEN AND MUSHROOM PIE
Serves 4–6

8 oz (225 g) flaky pastry or frozen puff pastry
1 boiling fowl, boiled, steamed or pressure cooked
4 oz (110 g) streaky bacon
4 oz (110 g) mushrooms, quartered
salt and freshly ground black pepper
1 tbsp chopped fresh parsley
chicken stock
beaten egg, to glaze

Preheat the oven to 450°F/230°C/Gas Mk 8. Make the pastry in the usual way, wrap in clingfilm and keep in the refrigerator until needed. Thaw if using frozen pastry. Remove the skin from the chicken, then pick off all the meat and cut it into bite-sized pieces. Roll up the bacon rashers. Mix the chicken, bacon and mushrooms, season and then add the chopped fresh parsley. Pack the meat mixture into a pie dish and half fill with chicken stock. Roll out the pastry to cover the top of the pie dish and brush the top with a little egg. Bake in the oven for about 30 minutes or until golden brown and risen.

CHICKEN LEMON CASSEROLE
Serves 6

6 chicken joints
salt and freshly ground black pepper
2 oz (50 g) butter
1 tbsp oil
1 onion, sliced
2 tbsp plain flour
½ pt (300 ml) chicken stock
1 lemon, peeled and sliced
2 bay leaves
1 tsp sugar

Preheat the oven to 375°F/190°C/Gas Mk 5. Wipe the chicken joints and sprinkle with salt and pepper. Heat the butter and oil in a frying pan and fry the joints quickly until golden brown all over. Transfer to a casserole. Add the onion to the frying pan and cook for about 5 minutes until soft. Sprinkle in the flour and cook for 1 minute. Pour in the stock and bring to the boil, stirring. Add the lemon, bay leaves, seasoning and sugar. Pour over the chicken. Cover and cook in the oven for about 45 minutes until the chicken is cooked. Remove the lid 15 minutes before the end of cooking time so that the joints brown.

CHICKEN JULIENNE
Serves 4

½ red pepper and ½ yellow pepper, deseeded and halved
6 oz (175 g) mangetout
1½ oz (35 g) butter
1½ oz (35 g) plain flour
½ pt (300 ml) rich chicken stock
½ pt (300 ml) milk
2 tbsp lemon juice
1 oz (25 g) cheese, grated
pinch dried rosemary
salt and freshly ground black pepper
1 lb (450 g) cooked chicken meat, cut in strips
1–2 tbsp chopped fresh parsley

Place the pepper halves under the grill until the skins are charred and start to blister, then remove the skins and cut the peppers into strips. Blanche the mangetout in boiling salted water for about 3 minutes, then drain. Melt the butter in a pan and stir in the flour. Cook gently, stirring, for a few minutes and then gradually add the chicken stock and milk, stirring well to avoid lumps. Bring the sauce to the boil, then simmer for about 3 minutes. Add the lemon juice, cheese and rosemary, and season to taste. Add the chicken, peppers and mangetout and simmer gently for a few minutes to heat through. Serve on a bed of rice and sprinkle with parsley.

HONEY-BASTED CHICKEN WINGS
Serves 4

3 tbsp soy sauce
3 tbsp lemon juice
2 slices fresh ginger root, grated
2 lb (900 g) chicken wings
3 tbsp honey
3 tbsp tomato ketchup
freshly ground black pepper

In a large shallow dish, mix together the soy sauce, lemon juice and ginger. Add the chicken wings, turn to coat thoroughly and leave to marinate overnight. Drain and mix 4 teaspoons of the marinade with the honey, tomato ketchup and plenty of pepper. Grill the chicken for 10 minutes, turning and basting with the honey mixture all the time. Continue to grill until cooked. Serve with noodles or boiled rice.

CHICKEN CASSEROLE
Serves 4

1 oz (25 g) butter
1 onion, sliced
1 garlic clove, sliced
4 oz (110 g) mushrooms, sliced
1 medium chicken, jointed
plain flour
2 tbsp oil
1 can mushroom soup
7 fl oz (200 ml) red wine
¼ pt (150 ml) double cream

Preheat the oven to 300°F/150°C/Gas Mk 2. Heat the butter in a pan, sauté the onion and garlic until soft but not browned, add the mushrooms and cook gently for another minute. Remove from the pan with a slotted spoon and place in a casserole dish. Dust the chicken pieces with flour. Heat the oil with the remaining fat in the pan and fry the chicken until evenly browned. Place the chicken on top of the onions and mushrooms and pour over the tin of mushroom soup. Cook in the oven for about 30 minutes, add the wine and cook for a further 30 minutes or until the chicken joints are cooked through and tender. Stir in the cream and reheat gently. Do not allow it to boil.

CHICKEN JAMBALAYA
Serves 4

6 tbsp oil
4 chicken joints
8 oz (225 g) ham, diced
1 green pepper, deseeded and chopped
2 onions, chopped
1 garlic clove, crushed
6 oz (175 g) long-grain rice
1 pt (600 ml) stock
8 oz (225 g) frozen peas
chopped pimentos, to garnish

Heat the oil and brown the chicken joints and ham. Add the green pepper, onions and garlic and fry gently, without browning, for 5 minutes. Add the rice and stock, season with salt and pepper, cover and simmer until cooked – about 20 minutes. Add the peas and simmer for 10 minutes. Garnish with pimentos to serve.

CHICKEN AND GREEN PEAS
Serves 4

4 chicken quarters
salt and freshly ground black pepper
4 slices streaky bacon, derinded and cut into strips
1 oz (25 g) butter
1 medium onion, chopped
2 oz (50 g) button mushrooms, sliced
1 tbsp plain flour
14 fl oz (400 ml) hot chicken stock
1 tsp dried mixed herbs
12 oz (350 g) fresh peas
fresh parsley sprigs, to garnish

Rinse the chicken in cold water and dry thoroughly. Rub salt and freshly ground black pepper into the meat. Sauté the bacon strips in a large, shallow, flameproof casserole over low heat until the fat runs and the bacon is cooked. Remove the bacon with a slotted spoon and keep aside. Add the butter to the casserole and put in the chicken, skin side down. Cook gently, turning frequently, for 10–15 minutes until evenly browned. Remove the chicken and keep aside. Reduce to low heat. Put the onion and mushrooms into the casserole and cook, stirring, until softened. Sprinkle in the flour, and stir to blend. Continue cooking for 1 minute. Gradually add the stock and the herbs and bring to the boil, stirring constantly. Replace the chicken and bacon in the casserole, cover and simmer over low heat for 50 minutes. Add the peas to the casserole, cover and simmer for a further 10 minutes or until the peas are cooked and the chicken is tender. Skim any fat off the top and add salt and freshly ground black pepper to taste. Serve garnished with the parsley.

CHICKEN BOURGUIGNON
Serves 8

6 lb (2.7 kg) chicken with giblets
1 tsp chopped fresh herbs
½ tsp mixed spice
salt and freshly ground black pepper
8 oz (225 g) streaky bacon rashers
2 medium onions, quartered
8 oz (225 g) button mushrooms
12 fl oz (350 ml) red wine
1 oz (25 g) butter
2 tbsp cornflour

Preheat the oven to 325°F/170°C/Gas Mk 3. Clean the inside of the chicken and remove the giblets. Sprinkle the herbs and spice inside the bird, and season to taste with salt and pepper. Cover the breast with over-lapping bacon rashers and place in a large roasting tin. Chop the chicken liver and heart and place in a saucepan. Chop the stalks from the mushrooms and add the onion, wine and mushroom stalks to the saucepan. Simmer over low heat for 15 minutes, then remove the onions with a slotted spoon. Keep the onions warm. Strain the wine and half the mushroom giblet stock over the chicken and cook in the oven for 3–3½ hours basting frequently. Half an hour before the end of cooking time, add the mushroom caps and the cooked onions to the roasting tin. When the chicken is cooked, transfer it to a warm serving dish together with the mushrooms and onions. Leave to stand for 10 minutes before carving. Strain the remaining mushroom giblet stock into a saucepan. Skim the fat from the roasting tin juices and add the juices to the pan with the butter. Mix the cornflour with a little water until blended and stir in the liquid. Boil until thickened, adjust seasoning as required and serve with the chicken.

HONEY ROAST DUCK
Serves 4

4 lb (1.8 kg) oven-ready duckling
2 tbsp cold water
salt
2 tbsp clear honey
1 tbsp boiling water
2–3 oranges, peeled and segmented
1 bunch watercress, to garnish
3–4 tbsp oil and vinegar dressing

Preheat the oven to 425°F/225°C/Gas Mk 7. Wipe the duckling and remove the giblets. Reserve the liver. Prick the skin all over and rub well with salt to crisp the skin. Place the duck on a rack in a roasting tin with the cold water. Roast for 20 minutes, then reduce the oven temperature to 350°F/180°C/Gas Mk 4 and cook at 25 minutes per 1 lb (450 g). After 1 hour roasting time, pour the duck fat from the tin. Blend the honey with the boiling water and baste the duck all over. Return to the oven to complete the roasting time, basting about three times with the honey mixture. When cooked leave the duck until completely cool. Cut into serving portions and arrange on a platter. Arrange orange segments around the duck with the watercress sprigs. Sprinkle the oil and vinegar dressing over the oranges and watercress.

FARMER'S FEAST
Serves 8

4½ lb (2 kg) chicken
8 oz (225 g) potatoes, peeled and sliced
8 oz (225 g) carrots, scraped and sliced
½ head of celery, cut into 1 in (2.5 cm) pieces
½ cauliflower, cut into florets
2 leeks, trimmed and cut into 1 in (2.5 cm) pieces
8 oz (225 g) frozen peas and sweetcorn
8 oz (225 g) frozen beans
Cheese sauce:
2 oz (50 g) butter
2 oz (50 g) plain flour
½ pt (300 ml) milk
½ pt (300 ml) chicken stock
salt and freshly ground black pepper
½ tsp dry English mustard powder
5 oz (150 g) grated cheese
3 tbsp breadcrumbs

Boil the chicken for about 1 hour, or until tender. Remove from the pan and reserve the stock. Skin and bone the chicken and chop the flesh into bite-sized pieces. Put the skin and bones back into the stock, bring to the boil and simmer for a further 30 minutes then strain. Add the potatoes to the stock, boil for 20 minutes, remove and keep warm. Blanch the remaining vegetables in some of the boiling stock. Do not overcook. Strain and measure out 1/2 pint (300 ml) of the liquid. (Use the remaining stock for soup or other chicken dishes.) Heat the oven to 375°F/190°C/Gas Mk 5. Make the cheese sauce: heat the butter and stir in the flour, add the milk and stock, stirring or whisking to avoid lumps. Add salt, pepper and mustard and half the cheese. Stir the sauce until thick and smooth. Put a layer of vegetables in a shallow ovenproof dish and cover with the chopped cooked chicken. Pour the cheese sauce over, sprinkle with the remaining cheese and breadcrumbs and bake in the oven for 40 minutes.

DUCK WITH TURNIPS
Serves 4

3–4 lb (1.4–2 kg) duckling
4 oz (110 g) butter
12 small onions
2 lb (900 g) small turnips, peeled
2 tsp sugar

Wipe over the duck and remove giblets. Rub salt and freshly ground black pepper inside the duck. Melt half the butter in a flameproof casserole, and brown the duck on both sides. Add the onions, salt and pepper to taste, cover and simmer over low heat for 1 hour, turning the duck often. Cut turnip into pieces. Melt the remaining butter in a frying pan and gently sauté the turnips for 10 minutes, then add 3½ fl oz (100 ml) of water. Season with salt and cover the frying pan. Simmer over low heat for 20 minutes, sprinkle in the sugar and cook for a further 10 minutes. Allow the turnip pieces to caramelise on all sides by shaking the pan frequently. When the duck is cooked, add the turnips to the casserole and simmer for 5 minutes. Place the duck on serving dish and surround with the onions and turnips. Pour over the cooking liquid and serve at once.

CHICKEN AND PEA CASSEROLE
Serves 4

4 chicken legs
salt and freshly ground black pepper
ground paprika
2–3 tbsp oil
1 lb (450 g) shelled fresh peas
1 pt (600 ml) beef stock
½ oz (10 g) butter
1 tbsp plain flour
¼ pt (150 ml) double cream
1 egg, separated
some grated nutmeg
2 tbsp chopped fresh parsley
1 lb (450 g) cooked long-grain rice

Preheat the oven to 425°F/220°C/Gas Mk 7. Sprinkle salt, pepper and paprika over the chicken legs. Heat the oil in a frying pan and fry the chicken legs until crisp. Place in a casserole dish. Pour the stock into a saucepan, add the peas and bring to the boil. Lower heat and simmer for 15 minutes until nearly tender. Drain well and reserve half the amount of stock. Melt the butter in a pan, gradually stir in the flour and cook for 2 minutes. Gradually pour in the reserved stock, stirring constantly. Mix together the cream and egg yolk and stir this into the sauce. Remove pan from heat and add some nutmeg. Thoroughly whisk the egg white until to stiff peak stage and fold into the sauce together with the parsley. Place the peas and rice into the casserole dish and mix well with the chicken legs. Spoon the sauce over the top and cook in oven for 15 minutes until top is golden brown

CORONATION CHICKEN
Serves 8

5 lb (2.3 kg) chicken, cooked
1 oz (25 g) butter
1 small onion, finely chopped
1 tbsp curry paste
1 tbsp tomato purée
4 fl oz (125 ml) red wine
1 bay leaf
juice of ½ lemon
4 canned apricots, drained and finely chopped
½ pt (300 ml) mayonnaise
¼ pt (150 ml) whipping cream
salt and freshly ground black pepper

Remove the flesh from the cooked chicken and cut the chicken flesh
into cubes. Melt the butter in a small saucepan and fry the onion for
3 minutes until soft. Stir in the curry paste, tomato purée, wine, bay
leaf and lemon juice. Simmer over low heat for 10 minutes until well
reduced. Strain and cool. Press the chopped apricots through a sieve
into a bowl. Beat in the curry sauce and the mayonnaise. Whisk the
cream until fairly stiff and fold into the mixture. Season with salt and
freshly ground black pepper to taste. Mix the chicken cubes into the
sauce and arrange on a dish. Garnish with lemon wedges.

CHICKEN LIVER GOUGÈRE
Serves 4

¼ pt (150 ml) water
2 oz (50 g) butter
2½ oz (60 g) plain flour
2 eggs
salt and freshly ground black pepper
Filling:
1 oz (25 g) butter
4 oz (110 g) chicken livers
1 onion, sliced
4 oz (110 g) mushrooms, sliced
1 tbsp plain flour
¼ pt (150 ml) stock
1 tomato, peeled and chopped
1 oz (25 g) Cheddar cheese, grated

Preheat the oven to 400°F/200°C/Gas Mk 6. Place the water and butter in a saucepan and bring to the boil. Remove from the heat and pour in the flour all at once. Beat very lightly. Cool slightly, then beat in the eggs and beat hard for 3 minutes. Season with salt and pepper and spoon into a greased ovenproof dish making a hollow in the centre. To make the filling, melt half the butter in a saucepan and sauté the chicken livers for 5 minutes on a high heat, then remove. Add the remaining butter and soften the onion on a low heat for about 10 minutes. Add the mushrooms, then stir in the flour. Cook gently for about 1 minute. Gradually stir in the stock, season and simmer for 5 minutes. Take the pan off the heat and add the livers and tomato. Pour the filling into the centre of the gougère in the ovenproof dish, sprinkle with cheese and bake for 10 minutes. Increase the temperature to 425°F/220°C/Gas Mk 7 and bake until crisp and brown – about 30 minutes.

CHICKEN, LEEK AND HAM FLAN
Serves 4–6

1 oz (25 g) butter
1 tbsp olive oil
1 lb (450 g) leeks, trimmed and thinly sliced
4 tbsp chicken stock
6 tbsp single cream
3 eggs
6 oz (175 g) cooked chicken, chopped
2 oz (50 g) smoked ham, chopped
salt and freshly ground black pepper
8 oz (225 g) ready-made shortcrust pastry
1 oz (25 g) fresh breadcrumbs

Preheat the oven to 400°F/200°C/Gas Mk 6. Place the butter and oil in a heavy-based saucepan over low heat, add the leeks and cook for 5 minutes, stirring from time to time. Pour in the stock, cover and cook over low heat for 5 minutes. Remove from the heat and transfer to a large bowl. Add the cream, eggs, chicken, ham and salt and pepper to the leeks and mix well. Roll out the pastry on a flat floured surface and use to line a 9 inch (23 cm) fluted flan ring. Stand the flan ring on a thick baking sheet and chill in the refrigerator for about 5 minutes. Arrange the chicken filling mixture in the flan case, sprinkle the breadcrumbs over the top and bake in the oven for 15 minutes then turn the heat down to 325°F/170°C/Gas Mk 3 for 15–20 minutes or until the flan is set and golden brown.

CHICKEN WITH BACON DUMPLINGS
Serves 4

1 tbsp olive oil
3½ lb (1.6 kg) chicken, cut into small pieces
2 large onions, chopped
1 garlic clove, crushed
1 oz (25 g) plain flour
1 pt (600 ml) chicken stock
1 bay leaf
salt and freshly ground black pepper
Dumplings:
8 oz (225 g) self-raising flour
pinch of salt
1 oz (25 g) butter
4 oz (110 g) shredded suet
4 oz (110 g) streaky bacon, rind removed and finely chopped
1 small onion, finely chopped
pinch dried thyme
1 egg, beaten
milk
1½ pt (900 ml) chicken stock

Heat the oil in a flameproof casserole. Add the chicken, onions and garlic and fry until lightly browned. Sprinkle over the flour and cook, stirring, for 1 minute. Stir in the stock, add the bay leaf and season to taste. Simmer for 1 hour or until tender. Make the dumplings: sift the flour and salt into a mixing bowl and rub in the butter. Mix in the suet, bacon, onion, thyme, egg and enough milk to make a soft but not sticky dough. Roll into small dumplings. Bring the stock to the boil in another saucepan. Drop in the dumplings, cover and poach for 20–25 minutes or until puffed up and cooked through. Transfer to the chicken mixture, using a slotted spoon. Remove the bay leaf. Serve from the casserole.

DUCK À L'ORANGE
Serves 4

4–5 lb (2–2.5 kg) duck
salt and freshly ground black pepper
juice of ½ lemon
¼ pt (150 ml) white wine
2 oz (50 g) butter
3–4 oranges, peeled and sliced across

Wipe over the duck with a clean, damp cloth and then rub thoroughly with salt and freshly ground black pepper. Pour the lemon juice and wine into a large plastic freezer bag, put the duck in the bag and leave for several hours, turning from time to time. Preheat the oven to 375°F/190°C/Gas Mk 5. Remove the duck (retaining the liquid) to a roasting tin, dot the butter all over and cook, allowing 20 minutes per pound, until the duck is tender, basting frequently with the liquid. Remove from the tin, leave to stand for 10 minutes, cut into portions and place on a hot serving dish. Skim the fat from the pan juices and pour the juices over the duck portions. Arrange the orange slices around the duck and serve immediately.

MEDITERRANEAN CHICKEN CASSEROLE
Serves 4

4 oz (110 g) haricot beans, soaked overnight
salt and freshly ground black pepper
2 tbsp olive oil
4 chicken legs
4 oz (110 g) gammon, cut into strips
4 oz (110 g) small onions, quartered
2 garlic cloves, crushed
2 tbsp plain flour
¾ pt (450 ml) chicken stock
3 oz (75 g) button mushrooms
1 red pepper, deseeded and diced
4 tomatoes, peeled and chopped
4 fl oz (125 ml) red wine (optional)
2 oz (50 g) green olives, stoned
1 bay leaf
1 tbsp chopped fresh parsley

Preheat the oven to 350°F/180°C/Gas Mk 4. Place the beans in a saucepan of boiling salted water and boil for about 30 minutes, then drain well. Heat the oil in a flameproof casserole, and fry the chicken, quickly, stirring until sealed on all sides. Remove from the casserole. Place the gammon and onions in the casserole and cook until golden. Add the garlic and flour and gradually pour in the stock, stirring constantly. Cook for 2 minutes until thick. Return the chicken to the casserole together with the beans, mushrooms, pepper, tomatoes, wine, olives, bay leaf and salt and pepper to taste. Bring to the boil, cover and cook in the oven for 45 minutes or until the chicken is tender. Sprinkle with parsley.

TARRAGON CHICKEN BREASTS
Serves 6

3 oz (75 g) butter
6 chicken breast fillets, skinned
1 oz (25 g) plain flour
¾ pt (450 ml) chicken stock
2 tbsp tarragon vinegar
2 tsp French mustard
½ tsp dried tarragon
3 tbsp grated Parmesan cheese
salt and freshly ground black pepper
¼ pt (150 ml) single cream

In a frying pan, heat 2 oz (50 g) of the butter and add the chicken breasts. Cover and cook over low heat for 20 minutes, turning once, until tender. Remove the chicken, drain and place on a warm serving dish. Add the remaining butter to a small saucepan, stir in the flour and gradually add the stock and vinegar. Stir in the mustard, tarragon and cheese and bring to the boil. Add salt and pepper to taste, lower the heat and simmer for 3 minutes. Remove the saucepan from the heat and stir in the cream. Return to low heat for 1 minute, stirring constantly. Pour over the chicken and serve at once.

CHICKEN FRIED WITH SPINACH
Serves 4–6

8 chicken thighs
1 medium onion, halved
1 carrot
salt and freshly ground black pepper
2 coriander seeds, crushed
4 garlic cloves, crushed
2 tsp salt
4 oz (110 g) butter
1 lb (450 g) fresh spinach, chopped

Just cover the chicken with water and simmer in a pan with the onion, carrot and seasoning for about 50 minutes. Remove the chicken, discard the onion and carrot and reserve the stock. Combine the coriander, garlic and salt and crush to a paste. Melt the butter and stir in the paste, then add the chicken. Sauté the pieces, turning until coloured all over. Add the spinach and cook until tender then adjust the seasoning. Serve with the hot stock separately, and rice.

SAVOURY CHICKEN LOAF
Serves 4

3 lb (1.4 kg) chicken, skinned
4 oz (110 g) streaky bacon rasher, rind removed, minced
8 oz (225 g) beef sausage meat
1 onion, minced
1 tsp dried mixed herbs
2 garlic cloves, crushed
3 fl oz (75 ml) dry cider
2 bay leaves

Preheat the oven to 325°F/170°C/Gas Mk 3. Remove the meat from the chicken and mince it. Mix with the bacon, sausage meat, onion, herbs, garlic and cider. Turn into a well-greased 2 lb (900 g) loaf tin, put the bay leaves on top and cover with foil. Stand in a roasting tin with at least 1 inch (2.5 cm) boiling water in the base. Bake for 2½ hours. Leave to cool, then chill before serving.

TURKEY WITH APRICOTS
Serves 4

1 lb (450 g) white turkey meat
2 tbsp plain flour
salt and freshly ground black pepper
1 tbsp cooking oil
1 oz (25 g) butter
1 lb (450 g) canned apricot halves
2 tbsp Worcestershire sauce
2 tbsp vinegar
2 tbsp demerara sugar
2 tbsp fresh lemon juice
¼ pt (150 ml) water

Cut the turkey into cubes. Toss the turkey in a bowl containing the flour and salt and pepper and make sure all the pieces are well covered in the flour mixture. Heat the oil and butter in a flameproof casserole dish and fry the turkey until brown on all sides, stirring frequently. Drain the apricots and chop coarsely. Place ¼ pt (150 ml) of the apricot juice in a bowl and add the Worcestershire sauce, vinegar, demerara sugar, lemon juice and water. Add any remaining seasoned flour to the casserole, then stir in the apricot juice mixture. Stir gently, bring to the boil, add the apricots, cover and simmer over low heat for 45 minutes until the turkey is tender.

CHICKEN WITH MACARONI
Serves 4

4 chicken quarters
1 small onion
1 tsp mixed herbs
1½ chicken stock cubes
1 pt (600 ml) water
6 oz (175 g) macaroni
Sauce:
8 fl oz (250 ml) milk
1 oz (25 g) plain flour
1 oz (25 g) butter
1 egg yolk, beaten
salt and freshly ground black pepper

Put the chicken quarters, whole onion, herbs and crumbled stock cubes in a large saucepan and pour in the water. Bring to the boil, reduce the heat, cover the pan and simmer for 45 minutes. Remove from the heat, lift out the chicken quarters and carefully remove the flesh from the bones. Discard the skin and bones. Take ¾ pt (450 ml) of the cooking liquid and make it up to 1 pt (600 ml) with water. Pour this in to another saucepan, add the macaroni and bring to the boil. Lower the heat and simmer for 12–15 minutes until the macaroni is tender. Meanwhile, add the milk to the remaining chicken cooking liquid. Stir, then add the chicken flesh and simmer for 15 minutes. Remove the chicken and keep hot. Blend the butter and flour together until smooth and add a little at a time to the milk stock liquid, stirring constantly. Add the egg yolk to the sauce. Cook over low heat until thick and season to taste with salt and pepper. When the macaroni is cooked, drain and transfer to a serving dish. Arrange the chicken on top and pour over the sauce. Serve at once.

BRAISED CHICKEN BREASTS WITH ONIONS
Serves 4

3 oz (75 g) butter
2 bunches spring onions, trimmed
4 boneless chicken breasts
fresh grated nutmeg
8 fresh sage leaves
1 pt (600 ml) milk
1 bay leaf
1 thyme sprig
1 clove

Melt the butter in a casserole over a low heat. Gently sauté the onions, turning them frequently for about 20 minutes. Cut each chicken breast into 2 slices and season with salt, pepper and nutmeg. Place a sage leaf at one end of each breast and roll it up like a cigar. Secure each roll with a wooden cocktail stick. Put the milk in a small pan and add the bay leaf, thyme, clove and seasoning. Bring to the boil then simmer gently for 10 minutes. After the onions have been cooking for 20 minutes, add the chicken rolls and brown lightly. Strain the hot milk into the casserole, cover and simmer over a low heat for 25 minutes, stirring from time to time. When cooked, the sauce should be thick and golden. If not, remove the lid and simmer a little longer until reduced. Serve hot.

TURKEY ITALIENNE
Serves 4–6

8 oz (225 g) tagliatelle
8 oz (225 g) button mushrooms, sliced
2 oz (50 g) butter
squeeze of lemon juice
1 oz (25 g) plain flour
1 pt (600 ml) hot turkey or chicken stock
salt and freshly ground black pepper
¼ pt (150 ml) double cream
2 tbsp dry sherry
1 lb (450 g) cold roast turkey, cut in 1 in (2.5 cm) chunks
1 oz (25 g) white breadcrumbs
1 oz (25 g) grated Parmesan cheese

Preheat the oven to 375°F/190°C/Gas Mk 5. Cook the tagliatelle in boiling salted water until just *al dente*. Sauté the sliced mushrooms in half the butter for about 5 minutes, add a squeeze of lemon juice and set on one side. Melt the remaining butter in a saucepan, stir in the flour and cook gently for 1 minute. Gradually add the hot stock, stirring all the time, until a smooth sauce is obtained. Simmer for about 3 minutes, season to taste and add the cream and sherry off the heat. Put the noodles in a buttered ovenproof dish. Add a little hot sauce and the mushrooms and toss together with a fork. Add the turkey chunks to the remaining sauce and pour over the noodles. Mix the breadcrumbs and grated cheese together and sprinkle over the top. Bake for about 20 minutes or until the top is crisp and golden.

CHEESE AND ANCHOVY CHICKEN
Serves 6

2 oz (50 g) can anchovy fillets in oil
a little milk
2 tbsp onion, finely chopped
1 tsp lemon juice
6 chicken breasts, on the bone
8 oz (225 g) Mozzarella cheese, sliced

Reserve 1 tablespoon of the anchovy fillet oil. Discard the remaining oil and place the anchovies in a shallow dish. Pour over milk to cover and leave for 20–30 minutes. Drain thoroughly, pat dry with kitchen paper and chop finely. Place the reserved oil in a saucepan and add the anchovies and onion. Cook for 5 minutes until a paste is formed. Stir in the lemon juice, remove from the heat and set aside to cool. Lift up the skin of each chicken breast and rub equal amounts of the anchovy paste onto the flesh of each. Replace the skin and cook under a moderate grill, with chicken skin face down on rack, for 35–45 minutes, turning once, until tender. Place a slice of cheese on each chicken breast and cook for 5 minutes.

APPLE AND POTATO CHICKEN
Serves 4–6

4 medium potatoes, sliced
2 apples, sliced
salt and freshly ground black pepper
4–6 chicken joints
2 oz (50 g) butter or margarine
1 large onion, sliced
14 oz (400 g) can chopped tomatoes
1 tsp brown sugar
1 tsp mustard
1 tbsp plain flour

Preheat the oven to 350°F/180°C/Gas Mk 4. Place the potatoes in a buttered casserole, season lightly and cover with apples. Season the chicken, heat the fat in a heavy saucepan, and fry the chicken until lightly browned all over. Remove from the pan. Add the onion and brown lightly, then add the tomatoes, sugar, mustard and flour and heat gently, stirring. Pour over the apples. Place the chicken pieces on top, cover and cook for about 1½ hours or until tender.

CHICKEN FLORENTINE
Serves 4

1 lb (450 g) fresh spinach
salt and freshly ground black pepper
4 boneless chicken breasts, skinned
3 oz (75 g) butter or margarine
1 tbsp oil
¼ tsp freshly grated nutmeg
1 oz (25 g) plain flour
¼ pt (150 ml) milk
4 oz (110 g) Cheddar or Double Gloucester cheese, grated
pinch mace
paprika

Preheat the oven to 375°F/190°C/Gas Mk 5. Wash the spinach, put into a pan with a pinch of salt and cook over low heat for 7 minutes until just tender. Drain well. Meanwhile, cut each chicken breast in two horizontally. Melt 1 oz (25 g) of the fat in a frying pan with the oil. Fry the chicken for 3 minutes on each side. Chop the spinach and mix with half the remaining fat, the nutmeg and salt and pepper to taste. Put the spinach in an ovenproof dish and arrange the chicken on top. Melt the remaining fat in a small pan. Add the flour and stir for 2 minutes. Gradually add the milk, then three-quarters of the cheese, the mace and seasoning. Simmer until thick. Pour over the chicken, then sprinkle with the remaining cheese and a little paprika. Bake for 30 minutes.

CURRIED TURKEY JOINTS
Serves 4

4 turkey leg joints
1 tsp curry powder
2 tbsp dry mustard powder
2 tsp Worcester sauce
salt and freshly ground black pepper

Preheat the oven to 350°F/180°C/Gas Mk 4. Remove the skin from the turkey and score the flesh. In a bowl, mix together the curry powder, mustard, Worcester sauce and salt and pepper to taste. Dip each turkey joint into the mixture until well coated, place in a shallow baking dish and cook in the oven until brown and the meat is tender.

CHICKEN LIVER RISOTTO
Serves 4

2 tbsp oil
1 onion, chopped
2 rashers streaky bacon, chopped
10 oz (300 g) long-grain rice
1 pt (600 ml) chicken stock
1 oz (25 g) margarine
4 oz (110 g) mushrooms, sliced
8 oz (225 g) chicken livers
chopped fresh parsley, to garnish
grated cheese, to serve

Heat the oil in a large saucepan and fry the onion and bacon until softened. Add the rice and cook, stirring, until golden. Pour in the stock, bring to the boil, cover tightly and simmer for 15 minutes. Do not lift the lid until the end of the cooking time, when all the liquid will have been absorbed and the rice will be tender. Meanwhile heat the margarine in a frying pan and cook the mushrooms and chicken livers until the livers are browned all over. Add to the cooked rice and reheat if necessary. Serve in a heated dish, garnished with parsley. Serve the cheese separately.

CHICKEN MARYLAND
Serves 4

1 young chicken, jointed; or 4 chicken joints
seasoned flour
beaten egg
fresh white breadcrumbs
3 oz (75 g) butter
1 tbsp oil
4 streaky bacon rashers
2 bananas, peeled and sliced lengthways
Corn Fritters (see page 129)

Skin the chicken. Roll in seasoned flour, brush with beaten egg and roll in breadcrumbs until well coated. Put in the refrigerator for 15 minutes. Heat the butter and oil in a large frying pan and sauté the chicken pieces until evenly browned and well cooked through. Keep hot. Grill the bacon rashers and roll up. Brown banana slices in the frying pan. Arrange the chicken on a heated serving dish together with the bacon rolls and fried bananas. Serve with Corn Fritters.

ROAST STUFFED DUCKLING
Serves 4

4 lb (1.8 kg) duckling
orange wedges, to garnish
Stuffing:
4 oz (110 g) white breadcrumbs
duck liver, minced
juice and grated rind of 1 orange
½ tsp dried sage
1 shallot, finely chopped
1 small egg, beaten
salt and freshly ground black pepper

Preheat the oven to 400°F/200°C/Gas Mk 6. Mix together all the stuffing ingredients and place in the neck of the duckling. Tuck up the flap and secure with a skewer or by sewing. Prick the skin and place on a rack in a roasting tin. Roast in the oven for 1½ hours or until cooked. Serve garnished with the orange wedges.

TURKEY LOAF BAKE
Serves 4

12 oz (350 g) cooked turkey, minced
4 oz (110 g) fresh breadcrumbs
½ tsp dry mustard powder
1 medium onion, finely chopped
3 oz (75g) mushrooms, finely chopped
½ tsp celery salt
2 tbsp chopped fresh parsley
2 eggs, beaten
¼ pt (150 ml) milk
1 tsp Worcester sauce
salt and freshly ground black pepper

Preheat the oven to 350°F/180°C/Gas Mk 4. Place the turkey, breadcrumbs, mustard, onion, mushrooms, celery salt and parsley in a large bowl. Mix well and add the eggs, milk and Worcester sauce. Continue to mix until all the ingredients are well blended, then add salt and pepper to taste. Place the mixture in a greased 2 lb (900 g) loaf tin and bake in the oven for 1 hour or until firm. Leave in the tin for about 5 minutes before turning out onto a serving dish. This can be eaten hot or cold.

TURKEY AND PORK RAGOUT
Serves 8

1½ lb (675 g) turkey escalopes
1½ lb (675 g) pork fillet
4 oz (110 g) butter
2 shallots, chopped
2 tbsp chopped fresh parsley
3 cloves garlic, crushed
½ tsp paprika
½ tsp coriander seeds
½ tsp caraway seeds
salt and freshly ground black pepper
1 pt (600 ml) water or chicken stock
3 medium onions, thinly sliced
6 tomatoes, skinned, deseeded and chopped
½ oz (10 g) plain cooking chocolate, melted

Dice the turkey and pork. Heat half the butter in a frying pan and cook the shallots, parsley and garlic until lightly browned. Add a quarter of the turkey and pork to the pan and cook until golden brown. Remove from the pan and place in a flameproof casserole dish. Fry all the remaining meat, several batches at a time, using the remaining butter if required and place in the casserole. Sprinkle the meat with paprika, coriander and caraway seeds. Add salt and pepper to taste. Pour over the water or stock, add the onions and cook gently over a low heat on top of the cooker. Preheat the oven to 375°F/190°C/Gas Mk 5. Add the tomatoes to the casserole and stir in the chocolate. Increase the heat and cook for 5 minutes until the chocolate has melted. Cover the casserole and cook in the oven for 1 hour or until the meat is tender.

TURKEY CRANBERRY CASSEROLE
Serves 4

4 x 6 oz (175 g) pieces raw turkey
seasoned flour
3 tbsp oil
2 celery stalks, strings removed
2 large onions, quartered
2 tbsp cornflour
½ pt (300 ml) chicken stock
8 oz (225 g) cranberry sauce
4 oz (110 g) mushrooms, quartered

Preheat the oven to 350°F/180°C/Gas Mk 4. Roll the turkey pieces in the seasoned flour. Heat the oil in a frying pan and fry the turkey until lightly browned. Drain and place in a casserole dish. Cut the celery into 1 inch (2.5 cm) lengths. Add the celery and onions to the frying pan and cook for 2–3 minutes. Remove with a slotted spoon and place on top of the turkey. Stir the cornflour into the frying pan and mix to a smooth paste. Gradually add the stock and cranberry sauce. Bring to the boil stirring constantly, then pour over the chicken and vegetables. Cover and cook in the oven for 1½–2 hours. Add the mushrooms 15 minutes before the end of the cooking time.

TURKEY SAUSAGE
Serves 6

2¼ lb (1 kg) turkey legs and breasts, skinned and boned
7 oz (200 g) ham
4 oz (110 g) stale bread, without crusts
3½ fl oz (100 ml) milk, warmed
4 oz (110 g) Gruyère cheese, grated
salt and freshly ground pepper
a little fresh nutmeg, grated
2 eggs
1 onion
1 clove
1 carrot
1 celery stalk
2 chicken stock cubes

Coarsely chop the turkey meat and finely chop the ham (alternatively chop in a food processor). Soak the bread in the milk and then mash it. Place turkey, ham, bread and cheese in a mixing bowl and season with salt and pepper and grated nutmeg. Add the eggs and mix well. Roll the mixture into a large sausage shape. Spike the onion with the clove. Bring 3½ pt (2 L) of water to the boil in a large saucepan and add the vegetables and stock cubes. Roll up the turkey sausage in a clean cloth, securing the ends with string. Place the roll into the saucepan containing the vegetables and stock and cook over low heat for 1¼ hours. Remove the sausage from the pan, leave to cool then remove the cloth and string. Cut into thick slices to serve.

TURKEY RISSOLES
Serves 4

6 oz (175 g) cooked turkey, finely minced
1 bacon rasher, derinded, crisply fried and crumbled
½ tsp mixed dried herbs
2 oz (50 g) fresh brown breadcrumbs
salt and freshly ground black pepper
1 egg yolk
1 egg, beaten
breadcrumbs for coating
oil for frying

Mix the turkey, bacon, herbs, breadcrumbs and seasoning with the egg yolk and bind the mixture together. Shape into small sausage shapes between floured hands and put in the refrigerator for 2 hours to firm up. Dip in the beaten egg and then roll in the breadcrumbs. Leave to firm up again for about 30 minutes. Heat the oil and fry the rissoles until golden brown. Drain well and serve with a green salad.

TURKEY AND RICE CASSEROLE
Serves 4

2 oz (50 g) butter
2 medium onions, chopped
8 oz (225 g) button mushrooms, sliced
8 oz (225 g) cooked turkey, diced
5 oz (150 g) stuffing, diced or crumbled
4 oz (110 g) ham, diced
2 tbsp finely chopped fresh parsley
thyme
salt and freshly ground black pepper
7 oz (200 g) long-grain rice
¾ pt (450 ml) hot turkey or chicken stock

Preheat the oven to 375°F/190°C/Gas Mk 5. Melt two-thirds of the butter in a large saucepan. Add the onions and cook for 5 minutes, stirring frequently. Add the mushrooms and cook for a further 5 minutes still stirring. Transfer the onions and mushrooms to a casserole dish and add the turkey, stuffing, ham, parsley and thyme. Add salt and pepper to taste. Stir well and set aside. In the same saucepan used to cook the onions and mushrooms, melt the remaining butter over low heat and add the rice. Cook, stirring, for 5 minutes. Stir the rice into the casserole. Pour in the hot stock, cover and cook in the oven for 40 minutes until the rice is tender.

LIZA'S PIE
Serves 4–6

8 oz (225 g) bacon rashers, rinds removed
8 oz (225 g) cooked turkey, cubed
4 oz (110 g) no-soak dried apricots, chopped
8 oz (225 g) pork sausage meat
salt and freshly ground black pepper
1 tablespoon dried mixed herbs (or leftover stuffing)
½ pt (300 ml) chicken stock
8 oz (225 g) shortcrust pastry
beaten egg, for glazing

Preheat the oven to 375°F/190°C/Gas Mk 5. Flatten the bacon rashers with a palette knife and put in a deep ovenproof dish. Put in a layer of turkey chunks and then a layer of apricots and finally a layer of sausage meat. Sprinkle the dried mixed herbs between each layer. Continue making layers until all the ingredients are used up, finishing with a layer of sausage meat. Pour over the stock. Roll out the shortcrust pastry to fit the top of the dish and cover the pie. Trim and flute the edges and decorate with pastry leaves. Make a slit in the top and brush with egg. Bake in the oven for 30 minutes or until the pastry is golden brown.

ROAST TURKEY WITH CELERY
Serves 4

2 celery hearts
4 garlic cloves
1¾ lb (800 g) turkey breasts
4 rashers smoked lean bacon
1 tbsp oil
½ tsp cinnamon
salt and freshly ground black pepper
4 tbsp brandy

Preheat the oven to 375°F/190°C/Gas Mk 5. Cut the celery hearts into thin slices. Grease an ovenproof dish and put in the celery slices and the whole garlic cloves. Roll together the turkey breasts and secure with string. Place on top of celery, then arrange the bacon slices on top of the turkey. Sprinkle all over with oil, cinnamon, salt and pepper and cook for 1¼ hours basting frequently. When cooked, remove from the oven and sprinkle with brandy which has been set alight.

CASSEROLE OF TURKEY WITH ONIONS
Serves 4

2¼ lb (1 kg) onions, thinly sliced
2 lb (900 g) legs and breast of turkey
2½ oz (60 g) butter
salt and freshly ground black pepper
9 fl oz (250 ml) beer

Place the onions in a large non-stick frying pan (without fat), cover the pan and sauté for 20 minutes over low heat, stirring occasionally. In the meantime, cut the turkey joints into chunks about 1 inch (2.5 cm) thick and discard the bones. Melt the butter in a frying pan and brown the turkey on all sides, seasoning with salt and pepper to taste. When the onions are cooked, add the turkey to the sauté pan and mix well. Pour over the beer, cover the pan and cook for 1 hour on low heat until there is no liquid left in the pan. Serve immediately.

RABBIT WITH PEAS
Serves 4

1 oz (25 g) butter
2½ lb (1.1 kg) rabbit, jointed into 8 pieces
salt and freshly ground black pepper
¼ pt (150 ml) dry white wine
1 onion, finely chopped
12 asparagus tips
1 sprig fresh tarragon
2 lb (900 g) frozen peas, thawed
pinch nutmeg
½ pt (300 ml) single cream
7 fl oz (200 ml) water

Melt the butter in a flameproof casserole over low heat. Add the rabbit pieces and cook until browned. Season with salt and freshly ground black pepper. Add the wine and continue cooking, turning the pieces over from time to time. When the wine has evaporated, add the onion, asparagus tips, tarragon, peas and nutmeg to the casserole. Stir in the cream and add the water. Cover and cook over a very low heat for 1 hour. Add more water during cooking if required.

RABBIT AND SAUSAGE BAKE
Serves 4

12 oz (350 g) sausage meat
1 rabbit, jointed
8 oz (225 g) onions, chopped
1 tbsp chopped fresh herbs
a little stock
salt and freshly ground black pepper
4 oz (110 g) fresh white breadcrumbs
1 oz (25 g) butter

Preheat the oven to 300°F/150°C/Gas Mk 2. Divide the sausage meat in half and place half in a flameproof casserole dish. Lay the rabbit joints on top, sprinkle with the onion and herbs, and add salt and pepper to taste. Spread the remaining sausage meat on top and half-fill the dish with stock. Cover with breadcrumbs and dot with butter. Cover the dish with foil and cook in the oven for 1¼ hours. Remove the foil and cook for a further 15 minutes to brown the top.

RABBIT AND PORK WITH TOMATOES
Serves 4

1 rabbit, jointed
1 oz (25 g) butter
4 oz (110 g) belly pork, cubed
1 garlic clove, crushed
2 onions, sliced
1 tsp basil
14 oz (400 g) can tomatoes
1 tbsp tomato purée
1 tsp sugar
salt and freshly ground black pepper

Preheat the oven to 325°F/170°C/Gas Mk 3. In a flameproof casserole dish, melt the butter and gently brown the rabbit and pork. Stir in the garlic, onions, basil and tomatoes and simmer over low heat for 10 minutes. Add the purée and sugar and stir well. Add salt and freshly ground black pepper to taste, cover and cook in the oven for 1½ hours.

TUDOR RABBIT
Serves 4

2½ lb (1.1 kg) rabbit, jointed
2 tbsp plain flour
2–4 tbsp oil
1 dessert apple, peeled, cored and sliced
4 oz (110 g) seedless green grapes
2 oz (50 g) raisins
1 medium orange, segmented
grated rind and juice of 1 orange
bouquet garni
1 onion, chopped
2 celery stalks, chopped
¼ pt (150 ml) red wine
6 tbsp chicken or vegetable stock
salt and freshly ground black pepper
fine strips of orange rind, to garnish

Preheat the oven to 325°F/170°C/Gas Mk 3. Roll the rabbit pieces in the flour. Heat the oil in a frying pan and fry the rabbit until brown. Transfer to a casserole dish and add the apple, grapes, raisins, orange segments, orange rind, juice and bouquet garni. Cook the onion and celery in the frying pan for 2–3 minutes with a little extra oil if required. Add the wine and stock, bring to the boil and then pour into the casserole dish. Cover and cook in the oven for 2 hours until the rabbit pieces are tender. Add salt and pepper to taste and remove the bouquet garni before serving. Garnish with the orange rind strips.

RABBIT CURRY
Serves 4

2–3 tbsp oil
1 large onion, chopped
1 tbsp hot curry powder
1 lb (450 g) rabbit, cooked and chopped
¾ pt (450 ml) chicken or vegetable stock
2 oz (50 g) lentils, boiled for 10 minutes
1 tbsp lemon marmalade
salt and freshly ground black pepper
1 oz (25 g) flaked almonds

Heat the oil in a frying pan and gently brown the onion. Stir in the curry powder and cook for 2 minutes. Stir in the rabbit and stock gradually. Drain the lentils and add to the pan. Stir in the marmalade and season with salt and freshly ground black pepper to taste. Cover the pan and simmer over low heat for 35–40 minutes until thickened. Mix in the almonds and serve immediately.

RABBIT STEW
Serves 4

1 rabbit, jointed
½ pt (300 ml) cider
2 onions, sliced
4 oz (110 g) ham, chopped
½ pt (300 ml) ham or chicken stock
1½ lb (675 g) potatoes, chopped
salt and freshly ground black pepper

Place the rabbit in a deep bowl, pour in the cider and leave for 8 hours. Place the rabbit, cider, onions, ham and stock in a large heavy saucepan. Season to taste with salt and pepper. Stir in the potatoes. Cover with a tight lid and cook over a very low heat for 2½–3 hours until the meat is tender. Test from time to time to ensure that the liquid has not dried out. If so add more stock. Alternatively cook in a low oven.

SAVOURY RABBIT FRY
Serves 6

1 rabbit, jointed
1 onion, sliced
¼ pt (150 ml) chicken or vegetable stock
1 lb (450 g) peeled or scraped potatoes
12 button onions
2 oz (50 g) dripping or 6 tbsp oil
2 bacon rashers
chopped fresh parsley
2 tsp plain flour
¼ pt (150 ml) chicken stock
2 tbsp tomato purée
4 tbsp red wine (optional)
salt and freshly ground black pepper

Wipe the rabbit joints and put in a saucepan with the onion and
chicken stock. Bring to the boil, lower the heat and simmer for
1 hour. Parboil the potatoes. Fry the button onions in the dripping or
oil until golden brown. Remove the rabbit joints from the stock and
fry until brown and the meat is tender. Arrange on a warmed serving
dish and keep hot. Cut the potatoes into slices and the bacon into
½ inch (1 cm) pieces and fry both in the remaining fat until cooked
and golden. Arrange the potatoes around the rabbit joints, together
with the button onions and bacon and sprinkle with chopped fresh
parsley. Stir the flour into the remaining fat and cook for 1 minute.
Gradually add the stock, tomato purée and wine; stir until a smooth
sauce is obtained and season to taste. Bring to the boil and simmer for
a few minutes. Strain into a sauceboat and serve separately.

MEAT

SAUSAGE MEAT ROLL
Serves 4–6

6 oz (175 g) self-raising flour
pinch salt
3 oz (75 g) shredded suet

Filling:
12 oz (350 g) sausage meat
2 apples, chopped
2 onions, chopped
1 tsp ground sage
salt and freshly ground black pepper

Preheat the oven to 375°F/190°C/Gas Mk 5. Sift the flour and salt into a bowl. Stir in the suet and add sufficient water to make a soft dough. Place on a flat floured surface and roll out into an oblong shape. Place the sausage meat, apples, onions, sage, and salt and freshly ground black pepper to taste in a bowl and mix well. Spread the mixture over the pastry leaving a border around the edges. Moisten the edges and roll up loosely. Place on a baking sheet and bake in the oven for 1 hour until the pastry is crisp and golden.

HAM AND CHEESE STUFFED TOMATOES
Serves 4

8 large tomatoes
salt and freshly ground black pepper
4 oz (110 g) Gouda cheese, cubed
4 oz (110 g) cooked ham, chopped
1 onion, chopped
1 tbsp chopped fresh parsley
½ oz (10 g) butter

Preheat the oven to 400°F/200°C/Gas Mk 6. Slice the top off each tomato and remove the seeds. Sprinkle the inside of each tomato with salt and pepper to taste. Place the cheese, ham, onion, and parsley in a bowl and mix thoroughly. Stuff the mixture into the tomatoes. Arrange the tomatoes in a greased ovenproof dish, place a dot of butter on top of each one and place the lids back on top of the tomatoes. Bake in the oven for 15 minutes and serve at once.

SAVOURY BACON PUDDING
Serves 4

8 oz (225 g) self-raising flour
salt and freshly ground black pepper
4 oz (110 g) shredded suet
Filling:
8–12 oz (225–350 g) streaky bacon
2 onions, chopped
2 tomatoes, chopped
2 carrots, diced
chopped fresh parsley

Put the flour and a pinch of salt in a bowl, mix in the suet and add sufficient water to make a soft dough. Roll out two-thirds of the pastry to line a 1½–2 pt (¾–1.2 L) pudding basin. Pile the bacon, onions, tomatoes, carrots and parsley in the basin, adding very little water. Add salt and pepper to taste. Roll out the remaining dough to form a lid which should be pressed down firmly on top of the pudding. Cover with greased greaseproof paper with a pleat across the top and secure the paper around the bowl with string. Place in a saucepan with boiling water and steam for 3 hours.

CARROT AND VEAL STEW
Serves 4

2 tbsp oil
1½ lb (675 g) stewing veal
1 onion, chopped
salt and freshly ground black pepper
1 tsp paprika
12 oz (350 g) carrots, cut into thin strips
2 tomatoes, peeled and cut into wedges
1 large gherkin, sliced
½ pt (300 ml) beef stock
1 tbsp chopped fresh parsley
½ tsp cayenne pepper

Heat the oil in a heavy-based saucepan, and fry the onion and veal until golden brown, adding salt and pepper to taste. Add the paprika and cook for 5 minutes, stirring from time to time. Add the carrots, tomatoes and gherkin and cook for 5 minutes. Pour in the stock and sufficient water to cover all the vegetables. Cover and cook over low heat for 1–2 hours, stirring occasionally. Sprinkle with parsley and cayenne pepper to serve.

LAMB AND PARSNIP STEW
Serves 6

1 oz (25 g) lard
1½ lb (675 g) stewing lamb, trimmed and cubed
1½ lb (675 g) parsnips, chopped
3 tomatoes, cut into wedges
1 onion, chopped
1 bay leaf
salt and freshly ground black pepper
1 pt (600 ml) beef stock
4 oz (110 g) streaky bacon, grilled and chopped or crumbled
2–3 tbsp single cream

Heat the lard in a large saucepan. Add the lamb, raise the heat and fry until the lamb is brown on all sides. Lower the heat and add the parsnips, tomatoes, onion, bay leaf and salt and pepper to taste. Pour in the stock and simmer gently for 40 minutes. Stir in the bacon and a little hot water if required and simmer for about 10 minutes. Stir in the cream and serve.

BACON AND COURGETTE BAKE
Serves 4

1 oz (25 g) butter
14 oz (400 g) courgettes, sliced
1 oz (25 g) streaky bacon, derinded and chopped
4 oz (110 g) cooked ham, cut into strips
4 oz (110 g) Emmenthal cheese, cut into strips

Egg topping:
2 eggs, beaten
4 tbsp milk
salt and freshly ground black pepper
paprika
1 tbsp chopped fresh parsley

Preheat the oven to 425°F/220°C/Gas Mk 7. In a frying pan, melt the butter, add the courgettes and cook for 4–5 minutes. Use a slotted spoon to remove the courgettes and arrange them in a 6 inch (15 cm) soufflé dish. Place the bacon in the pan and fry in the pan juices until crisp. Place the ham, cheese and fried bacon in a dish and mix thoroughly, then spread the mixture evenly over the courgettes. Mix together the eggs, milk, salt, pepper, paprika and parsley. Pour over the top of the courgettes and bake in the oven for 20 minutes until the top is crisp and golden brown. Serve at once.

BEEFY MEAT LOAF
Serves 4

1 lb (450 g) lean minced beef
3 oz (75 g) fresh brown breadcrumbs
1 medium onion, coarsely grated
2 carrots, grated
1 egg, lightly beaten
salt and freshly ground black pepper
2 tbsp chopped fresh parsley

Preheat the oven to 350°F/180°C/Gas Mk 4. Mix all the ingredients in a large bowl until well blended. Pile the mixture into a 1 lb (450 g) loaf tin and level the top. Bake in the oven in a roasting tin with 1 inch (2.5 cm) boiling water in the bottom for 1¼ hours until the juices run out clear when a skewer is inserted in the loaf. Turn out onto a serving dish. This can be served hot or cold.

SAVOURY MEAT LOAF
Serves 4

1 lb (450 g) stewing lamb, trimmed and minced
2 cloves garlic, crushed
3 tbsp chopped fresh herbs (mint, oregano, thyme)
3 oz (75 g) fresh brown breadcrumbs
1 medium onion, coarsely grated
2 carrots, grated
1 egg, lightly beaten
salt and freshly ground black pepper
2 tbsp chopped fresh parsley

Preheat the oven to 350°F/180°C/Gas Mk 4. Mix all the ingredients in a large bowl until well blended. Pile the mixture into a 1 lb (450 g) loaf tin and level the top. Bake in the oven in a roasting tin with 1 inch (2.5 cm) boiling water in the bottom for 1¼ hours until the juices run out clear when a skewer is inserted in the loaf. Turn out onto a serving dish.

IRISH STEW
Serves 4

1½ lb (675 g) neck of lamb, chopped
12 oz (350 g) onions, sliced
¾ pt (450 ml) water
1 lb (450 g) medium potatoes, peeled

Place the lamb, onions and water in a large saucepan and bring to the boil. Remove any scum from the water, lower the heat and simmer gently for 1¼ hours. Add the potatoes and simmer for 40 minutes or until the potatoes are cooked. Season to taste with salt and pepper.

BEEF AND BEER STEW WITH DUMPLINGS
Serves 6

2 tbsp oil
3 oz (75 g) streaky bacon, diced
2 large onions, chopped
6 peppercorns
2 carrots, chopped
2 celery stalks, chopped
2 lb (900 g) chuck steak, trimmed and cubed
7½ oz (200 g) can prunes
12 fl oz (350 ml) lager
1 tsp German mustard
1 tbsp sugar
salt and freshly ground black pepper
Dumplings:
4 oz (110 g) stale rye or coarse brown bread
3 fl oz (75 ml) milk, heated
½ oz (10 g) butter
1 small onion, finely chopped
1 tbsp fresh parsley, chopped
1 egg, lightly beaten
pinch nutmeg
1 oz (25 g) plain flour

Heat the oil in a large saucepan and fry the bacon, onions and peppercorns for 2–3 minutes. Mix in the carrots, celery and meat and fry until the meat is well sealed. Add the prunes, beer, mustard, sugar, and seasoning to taste. Bring to the boil, then simmer for 2 hours, stirring occasionally. Meanwhile prepare the dumplings: soak the bread in the milk for 1 hour. Melt the butter in a small pan and fry the onion until golden. Transfer the onion to the bread and milk mixture and stir in the parsley, egg and nutmeg. Add the flour, mixing well with salt and pepper to taste. Using floured hands, form the mixture into six small balls and drop into a saucepan of simmering water for 10–15 minutes until cooked through. Place on top of the stew to serve.

STUFFED MARROW RINGS
Serves 4

1 x 2 lb (900 g) marrow
1 tbsp oil
1 onion, chopped
4 oz (110 g) mushrooms, chopped
1 oz (25 g) fresh breadcrumbs
2 tomatoes, skinned and chopped
1 tbsp chopped fresh parsley
1 tbsp fresh basil, chopped
8 oz (225 g) lean minced beef
salt and freshly ground black pepper

Preheat the oven to 350°F/180°C/Gas Mk 4. Slice the marrow cross-wise into 2 inch (5 cm) rings. Remove and discard the seeds. Arrange the marrow rings in a lightly greased baking dish. Heat the oil in a frying pan and cook the onion gently for 3 minutes, stirring from time to time. Stir in the mushrooms and cook for 3 minutes. Remove from the heat and mix thoroughly with the breadcrumbs, parsley, basil and salt and pepper to taste. Meanwhile add the mince to the pan and fry until brown on all sides. Add to the bowl and mix well. Pile the mixture evenly into the centre of each of the marrow rings and cover the dish with foil. Bake in the oven for 20–30 minutes until the marrow is just soft. To vary this recipe, finely chopped cooked ham, cooked minced lamb or cooked minced chicken can be used in place of beef. Serve with a spicy tomato sauce

STEWED OXTAIL
Serves 4

4 tbsp oil
1 oxtail, cut into joints
seasoned flour
2 onions, sliced
2 carrots, sliced
1 turnip, sliced
2 celery stalks, chopped
4 cloves
bouquet garni
2 beef stock cubes
salt and freshly ground black pepper
1 pt (600 ml) hot water

Coat the joints in seasoned flour and fry in the hot oil until evenly browned all over. Remove from the pan with a slotted spoon, put in a large saucepan and keep warm. Add the vegetables and continue frying these for 2 minutes, turning them over in the fat. Add the vegetables to the meat, together with the cloves and bouquet garni. Season well and pour in the beef stock cubes dissolved in the hot water. Cover the saucepan, bring to the boil and gently simmer for 2–3 hours, or until the meat comes away from the bones. If the tail is very fatty, the dish can be cooked the day before and the hardened fat lifted off the next day. Bring the stew to the boil and let it simmer for 15 minutes before serving. If there is not enough meat, some stewing steak may be added to stretch the meal.

KIDNEY AND SAUSAGE CASSEROLE
Serves 4

8 oz (225 g) chipolata sausages, halved
1 oz (25 g) butter or margarine
6–8 lamb kidneys, skinned, halved and cored
1 large onion, chopped
½ oz (10 g) plain flour
½ pt (300 ml) stock
4 tbsp red wine or sherry (optional)
salt and freshly ground black pepper
½ tsp dried dill
2¼ lb (1 kg) potatoes, cooked and mashed
beaten egg or melted butter, to glaze
chopped fresh parsley, to garnish

Preheat the oven to 350°F/180°C/Gas Mk 4. Place the sausages in a flameproof casserole dish with the melted butter and fry until lightly browned. Remove from the casserole. Fry the kidneys until well sealed on all sides, then remove. Fry the onion until soft, stir in the flour and cook for 1 minute. Add the stock and wine or sherry gradually and bring to the boil. Replace the sausages and kidneys in casserole, season to taste and add the dill. Cover the casserole and cook in the oven for 30–40 minutes until tender. Meanwhile pipe or fork the potato around the edge of a shallow heatproof serving dish, brush the top of the potato with egg or butter and place under a hot grill or in the oven to brown. Pile the sausage and kidney mixture in the middle of the potato-lined dish and sprinkle with parsley.

SAVOURY LIVER
Serves 4

1 lb (450 g) lamb liver
2 oz (50 g) fresh white breadcrumbs
1 tbsp chopped fresh parsley
1 tsp mixed dried herbs
1 oz (25 g) shredded suet
grated rind of ½ lemon
salt and freshly ground black pepper
egg or milk, to mix
4 rashers streaky bacon, derinded
¼ pt (150 ml) stock or water

Preheat the oven to 350°F/180°C/Gas Mk 4. Wash and slice the liver and arrange in a casserole dish. Mix together in a bowl the breadcrumbs, parsley, herbs, suet, lemon rind and salt and pepper to taste. Bind with a little egg or milk. Spread the mixture on the liver and place the bacon on top. Pour in the stock or water. Cover and cook in the oven for 30–45 minutes until the liver is tender, removing the cover for the final 15 minutes to crisp the bacon.

LIVER AND BACON HOT POT
Serves 6

1 lb (450 g) lamb liver
seasoned flour
2 medium onions, sliced
1½ lb (675 g) cooking apples, sliced
12 oz (350 g) bacon, chopped, leaving 6 rashers whole
salt and freshly ground black pepper
12 oz (350 g) tomatoes, sliced
½ pt (300 ml) water

Heat the oven to 350°F/180°C/Gas Mk 4. Lightly dust the liver with seasoned flour. Heat some oil in a frying pan and sauté the onions gently until soft, add the apples and turn in the hot fat for a few moments. Remove both with a slotted spoon and place in the base of an ovenproof casserole. Add the chopped bacon to the pan and fry gently until the fat runs, then add the liver and seal on all sides. Place these on top of the onions. Season well. Lay the sliced tomatoes on the top and pour in just enough water to reach the top of the ingredients. Cover with the whole rashers of bacon and bake for 1 hour.

TRIPE AND ONIONS
Serves 4

1 lb (450 g) tripe, washed
8 oz (225 g) onions, sliced
salt and freshly ground black pepper
¾ pt (450 ml) milk
¼ oz (15 g) butter or margarine
¼ oz (15 g) plain flour
2 tbsp chopped fresh parsley

Preheat the oven to 135°F/70°C/Gas Mk ½. Place the tripe into cold water in a pan and bring to the boil. Remove from the water and cut into strips. Put the strips of tripe in a casserole dish covered with the slices of onion and season well. Bring the milk to the boil and pour over. Cover with a lid and cook for 3 hours. Strain off the liquor. Melt the butter in a small pan and add the flour. Stir for 1 minute and then gradually add the liquor from the casserole, stirring all the time. When thickened, boil gently for 5–10 minutes to cook the flour. Check the seasoning. Arrange the tripe and onions in the serving dish and strain the sauce over them. Sprinkle with parsley.

HERBED PORK MEAT BALLS
Serves 4–6

1½ lb (675 g) pig liver, chopped
¼ lb (110 g) pork, minced or diced
1 large onion, chopped
pinch each sage, thyme and basil
2 eggs, beaten
freshly grated nutmeg
breadcrumbs
salt and freshly ground black pepper

Put the meats, onion, and herbs into a saucepan and season well. Cover tightly with a lid and cook very slowly for 30 minutes, giving it a stir half way through to prevent burning. Heat the oven to 350°F/180°C/Gas Mk 4. Drain off the fat and let the mixture cool down. Mix in the eggs and a pinch of nutmeg, and stir in enough breadcrumbs to make a fairly stiff mixture. Shape into 3 inch (7.5 cm) balls and bake, covered with a lid of foil in a preheated oven for about 40 minutes, taking the foil off the tin for the last 15 minutes to brown. Serve with a rich brown gravy, creamed potatoes and peas.

BEEF AND SWEETCORN STEW
Serves 4

½ oz (10 g) lard
1 lb (450 g) stewing beef, cubed
2 large onions, chopped
1 carrot, chopped
1 pt (600 ml) beef stock
salt and freshly ground black pepper
1 tbsp paprika
12 oz (350 g) can sweetcorn
2½ oz (60 g) can tomato purée
¼ pt (150 ml) soured cream

Preheat the oven to 325°F/160°C/Gas Mk 3. Heat the lard in a flameproof casserole and when melted, add the beef and cook until browned on all sides. Add the onions and carrot and cook for 5 minutes. Gradually pour in the stock, stirring well. Add salt and pepper to taste and the paprika. Cover the casserole and cook in the oven for 1–1½ hours. Stir the sweetcorn and the juices from the can into the casserole, mixing well. Cover and cook for 30 minutes, stirring from time to time. Remove from the oven and blend in the tomato purée. Reheat on top of the cooker, but do not boil. Add the soured cream and serve at once.

FRIED SWEETBREADS
Serves 4

1 lb (450 g) lamb sweetbreads
juice of ½ lemon
1 egg, beaten
breadcrumbs for coating
oil for deep frying
tomato slices and onion rings, to garnish

Soak the sweetbreads in cold water for 3–4 hours, drain and place in a saucepan. Cover with cold water and lemon juice and slowly bring to the boil. Lower the heat and simmer for 5 minutes. Drain and leave in cold water until they are cold and firm. Strip off any unwanted tissues. Press the sweetbreads well between layers of absorbent kitchen paper, slice and dip first in the beaten egg, followed by the breadcrumbs. Fry in hot fat until golden brown. Place on a serving dish, garnish with tomato slices and onion rings. Serve immediately.

ITALIAN MEAT SAUCE
Serves 4–6

4 tbsp olive oil
2 onions, finely chopped
3 cloves garlic, crushed
1 carrot, grated or finely chopped
4 oz (110 g) chicken livers, finely chopped
1 lb (450 g) lean minced beef
28 oz (800 g) canned plum tomatoes
2 tbsp tomato pureé (optional)
¼ pt (150 ml) red wine (optional)
1 bay leaf
1 bouquet garni
6 fresh basil leaves, chopped or ½ tsp dried
½ pt (300 ml) beef stock

Heat 3 tablespoons oil in a heavy saucepan, turn the heat to low and sweat the onions and garlic for 3 minutes, then add the carrots and cook over a low heat for at least 6 minutes. Heat 1 tablespoon oil in a frying pan and brown the chicken livers and beef, turning over frequently with a wooden spoon or fork to separate the pieces. Tip into the saucepan with the vegetables, add the remaining ingredients, mix well and bring to the boil. Reduce the heat and simmer for at least 45 minutes stirring from time to time. Serve with pasta.

WELSH PORK CHOPS
Serves 4

4 pork loin chops, boned
4 oz (110 g) Emmenthal cheese, grated
6 pickled baby silverskin onions, halved
salt and freshly ground black pepper
1 tbsp chopped fresh parsley

Grill the pork chops under a preheated grill for about 7 minutes on each side or until the fat around the meat begins to brown. Two minutes before the end of cooking time divide the cheese equally between the four chops, sprinkling evenly on top of each. Arrange the halved silverskin onions on top of the cheese and return to the grill. Leave until the cheese is bubbling, season well and sprinkle with parsley.

NORMANDY CASSEROLE
Serves 6

1½ lb (675 g) pork sausages
1 large onion, sliced
1 tbsp fresh sage, chopped
1 tbsp fresh thyme, chopped
10 oz (300 g) can condensed tomato or mushroom soup
14 oz (400 g) can flageolet beans, drained
14 oz (400 g) can haricot beans, drained
14 oz (400 g) can butter beans, drained
salt and freshly ground black pepper

Cook the sausages under a preheated grill, turning over frequently until they are golden brown all over. Put a little oil or butter in the base of a large flameproof casserole and gently sauté the onion until beginning to soften. Add the sausages, cut into chunks, together with the herbs. Pour in the tomato or mushroom soup and gently stir in all the beans. Season to taste. Cover the casserole and simmer over a gentle heat for 20 minutes.

KIDNEY STEW WITH ONIONS
Serves 4

1 lb (450 g) pig kidneys
2 tbsp plain flour
salt and freshly ground black pepper
2 tbsp oil
4 rashers streaky bacon, chopped
4 onions, sliced
½ pt (300 ml) beef stock
pinch ground ginger
8 oz (225 g) pasta shapes

Wash the kidneys well, removing any skin and membranes. Snip out the cores with scissors. Slice the kidneys lengthwise. Season the flour with salt and pepper and coat the kidney halves. Heat the oil in a saucepan and fry the bacon and onions until soft. Add the kidneys and any excess flour and continue cooking for 2–3 minutes, stirring well. Add the stock and ginger and bring to the boil, stirring constantly. Cover and simmer gently for 1 hour. Meanwhile cook the pasta in a large saucepan of boiling salted water for 15 minutes or until just tender. Drain well and keep hot. To serve, put the pasta round the edges of a heated serving dish and pile the kidney stew in the centre.

LIVER AND BACON IN TOMATO SAUCE
Serves 6

1½ lb (675 g) lamb liver
2 oz (50 g) plain flour
salt and freshly ground black pepper
1 oz (25 g) margarine
1 onion, chopped
¾ pt (450 ml) tomato juice
6 rashers streaky bacon

Preheat the oven to 375°F/190°C/Gas Mk 5. Slice the liver into
½ inch (1 cm) slices. Put the flour onto a plate and season with salt
and pepper. Coat the slices of liver with the seasoned flour. Heat the
margarine in a flameproof casserole, add the onion and fry for
3–5 minutes or until soft but not browned. Add the liver and fry
lightly on both sides. Stir in the tomato juice and salt and pepper to
taste. Remove the rind from the bacon, cut the rashers in half and roll
them up. Place the bacon rolls on top of the casserole and bake,
uncovered, for 30 minutes.

BRAISED PORK KNUCKLES WITH APPLE
Serves 4

4 small pork knuckles
4 onions, sliced
3 carrots, sliced
1 bay leaf
1 clove
3 tbsp vinegar
1 oz (25 g) butter, melted
3 cooking apples, chopped into thick pieces
¼ pt (150 ml) apple juice

Place the pork knuckles in a large saucepan with the onions, carrots,
bay leaf and clove. Pour in the vinegar and enough water to cover.
Bring to the boil, then cover and simmer for 45 minutes. Preheat the
oven to 350°F/180°C/Gas Mk 4. Drain off the cooking liquid.
Remove the knuckles, brush with butter and arrange in a large
ovenproof dish. Add the cooked vegetables, seasonings, apple pieces
and juice. Cover and cook in the oven for 2 hours until the meat is
tender.

HEART CASSEROLE
Serves 4

4 small lamb hearts
4 oz (110 g) breadcrumbs
1 medium onion, finely chopped
3 tbsp melted butter
2 tsp mixed dried herbs
salt and freshly ground black pepper
2 tbsp seasoned flour
2 tbsp oil
1 pt (600 ml) stock
1 onion, sliced
4 celery stalks, sliced
4 oz (110 g) carrots, sliced

Preheat the oven to 350°F/180°C/Gas Mk 4. Wash the hearts, slice open, remove any tubes and wash again. To make the stuffing: mix together the breadcrumbs, onion, melted butter, herbs and salt and pepper to taste. Spoon the mixture into each heart and tie them into their original shape with string. Dip in seasoned flour and fry in hot oil until brown. Then place the hearts in casserole dish, pour in the stock, cover and cook in oven for 2½ hours, turning them frequently. Add the onion, celery and carrots for the last 1 hour of cooking time.

SPARE RIBS WITH BARBECUE SAUCE
Serves 4

8–16 pork spare ribs
1 oz (25 g) melted butter
salt and freshly ground black pepper

Sauce:
1 oz (25 g) butter
2 onions, sliced
1 garlic clove, crushed
4 oz (110 g) mushrooms
14 oz (400 g) can tomatoes
1 tsp Worcester sauce
1 tsp made mustard
½ tsp mixed dried herbs
½ tsp caster sugar

Brush the spare ribs with the melted butter and sprinkle with salt and freshly ground black pepper. Arrange under a hot grill and cook for 15–20 minutes, turning occasionally and lower the heat after 10 minutes. To make the sauce, place the butter in a frying pan and heat until melted. Add the onions, garlic and mushrooms and fry gently for a few minutes. Stir in the tomatoes, Worcester sauce, mustard, herbs, sugar and salt and pepper to taste and simmer gently over low heat for 10 minutes. Place the spare ribs on a warmed serving dish and pour over the sauce.

LIVER AND BACON SALAD
Serves 4

8 oz (225 g) lamb liver, thinly sliced
milk
2 tbsp seasoned flour
4 rashers streaky bacon
1 bunch spring onions, sliced
1 crisp lettuce
2 oz (50 g) pine kernels, toasted
1 small orange

Dressing:
¼ pt (150 ml) soured cream
4 tbsp groundnut oil
1 tsp Dijon mustard
salt and black freshly ground black pepper

Soak the liver in milk for 30 minutes. Drain on kitchen paper and dust with flour. Chop the bacon into 1 inch (2.5 cm) pieces and fry until crisp. Drain on kitchen paper. Add oil to the pan if there is not sufficient bacon fat, and sauté the liver for 4 minutes each side, or until just cooked. Peel the orange and remove all the pith with a sharp knife. Cut the segments out from the membrane and cut into half. Arrange the lettuce on plates with the spring onions, orange pieces and liver. Sprinkle the crisp bacon and pine kernels over the top. Whisk the dressing ingredients together and serve separately.

KIDNEY AND MUSHROOMS WITH TOAST
Serves 3–4

1 tbsp oil
2 rashers rindless streaky bacon, chopped
1 small onion, thinly sliced
6 lamb kidneys, skinned, quartered and cored
1 oz (25 g) plain flour
14 oz (400 g) can tomatoes
salt and freshly ground black pepper
8 oz (225 g) mushrooms
butter, melted
8 triangles of toast or fried bread

Heat the oil in a saucepan and fry the bacon gently. Add the onion
and kidneys and fry for a few minutes until lightly browned. Add the
flour, then stir in the tomatoes. Bring to the boil, season to taste,
reduce the heat and simmer for 10 minutes. Brush the mushrooms
with a little butter and grill for a few seconds. Turn the kidney
mixture into a hot dish and arrange the mushrooms down one side
and the triangles of toast or fried bread down the other.

DEVILLED KIDNEYS
Serves 4

8 lamb kidneys
2 oz (50 g) butter
4 tsp plain flour
1 tsp French mustard
1 tsp curry powder (optional)
¼ tsp Worcestershire sauce
4 fl oz (125 ml) stock or water
salt and freshly ground black pepper
squeeze of lemon juice
hot buttered toast, to serve

Skin the kidneys, halve and remove the cores, then cut into thin slices.
Heat half the butter in a frying pan. Quickly brown the kidneys on
both sides (this should only take about 1½ minutes), then transfer to a
heated dish. Add the flour, mustard and curry powder (if using) and
stir well. Add the Worcestershire sauce, stock or water and cook for
2 minutes. Season with salt, pepper and lemon juice. Add the
remaining butter and the kidneys and toss well until heated. There
should be very little sauce. Serve immediately on hot buttered toast.

LIVER WITH ORANGE SAUCE
Serves 4

1 lb (450 g) lamb liver
¼ pt (150 ml) skimmed milk
flour for dusting
salt and freshly ground black pepper
7 fl oz (200 ml) orange juice
¼ tsp chopped fresh thyme
¾ tsp arrowroot
orange slices and thyme sprig, to garnish

Wipe and slice the liver, cover with the milk and leave for 1–2 hours. Remove and pat dry with absorbent paper. Lightly dust with a little flour and dry-fry until lightly cooked. Season to taste, arrange in serving dish and keep hot. Heat the orange juice in a small pan with the thyme. Mix the arrowroot with a little water to make a smooth paste and pour into the juice. Bring to the boil, stirring constantly, until a smooth sauce is obtained. Pour the sauce over the liver and garnish with orange slices and thyme.

OX HEART CASSEROLE
Serves 4

1 ox heart
2 bacon rashers
4 button onions
plain flour
red wine or stock
bouquet garni
fried bread, to garnish

Heat the oven to 325°F/170°C/Gas Mk 3. Remove any gristle from the ox heart and cut into cubes. Chop the bacon rashers and fry very gently to release the fat; add the onions and cook until golden. Remove from the pan and keep on one side. Brown the cubes of heart all over in the bacon fat. Pour off excess fat and sprinkle in enough flour to coat the heart cubes, cook for 1 minute and then stir in enough red wine to make a smooth thin sauce. If liked, add half stock. Put in an ovenproof casserole together with the bouquet garni, bring to the boil, lower the heat, cover and simmer very gently for 1½ hours in the oven. Then add the button onions, cover the casserole and cook gently for a further 1½ hours. Serve garnished with triangles of fried bread.

STEAK AND KIDNEY PUDDING
Serves 4

8 oz (225 g) self-raising flour, sifted
4 oz (110 g) shredded suet
salt and freshly ground black pepper
Filling:
1 lb (450 g) stewing steak
2–3 lamb kidneys or 8 oz (225 g) ox kidney
2 small onions, finely chopped
½ oz (10 g) plain flour
stock or water
1 tsp Worcester sauce

Place the flour, suet and seasoning in a bowl, and mix with sufficient cold water to form a firm dough. Use most of the dough to line a greased pudding basin retaining some for the cover. Chop the steak into small pieces and skin, core and quarter the kidneys. Mix together and arrange in layers in the basin, sprinkling each layer of meat with flour, chopped onion and salt and pepper to taste. Pour in enough stock or water to nearly fill the basin. Cover with the crust lid pressing down the edges all round. Cover with greased greaseproof paper with a pleat across the top to allow the pastry to rise. Secure the paper around the basin with string. Place the basin in a large saucepan of boiling water and steam for 4 hours.

LIVER NORMANDY
Serves 4

1 lb (450 g) liver
milk
1 oz (25 g) plain flour
salt and freshly ground black pepper
1 tsp dry mustard powder
4 tbsp oil
2 medium cooking apples, peeled, sliced and cored
2 medium onions, sliced
6 rashers streaky bacon
½ pt (300 ml) water

Heat the oven to 350°F/180°C/Gas Mk 4. Cut the liver in thin slices and steep in milk for 30 minutes. Remove from the milk, pat dry and coat with a mixture of the flour, salt, pepper and mustard powder. Brown lightly in the hot oil on both sides. Fill a greased ovenproof casserole with alternate layers of liver, apples and onions and top with the rashers of bacon. Pour in the water, put the lid on the casserole and cook in the centre of a preheated oven for 1½ hours, removing the lid for the last 20 minutes. Serve with creamy mashed potatoes and spinach.

TONGUE AND LENTIL CASSEROLE
Serves 4

8 oz (225 g) lentils, soaked overnight
4 sheep tongues
1 oz (25 g) lard
2 onions, chopped
8 oz (225 g) carrots, chopped
pinch mixed dried herbs
1 garlic clove, crushed
salt and freshly ground black pepper

Place the tongues in a bowl of cold water and leave for 3–4 hours. Drain and place in a saucepan of fresh cold water. Bring to the boil, lower the heat and simmer for 10–15 minutes. Drain off the cooking liquid, replace with more fresh cold water and simmer for 1 hour. Drain, but reserve the liquid. Set aside the tongues to cool, remove the skin and cut into slices. Preheat the oven to 325°F/170°C/Gas Mk 3. Melt the lard in a frying pan and brown the onions. Place the onions together with the tongue slices in an ovenproof casserole dish. Gently fry the lentils and carrots in the pan for a few minutes, then add to the casserole. Stir in the herbs, garlic and salt and pepper to taste and pour in the reserved cooking liquid from the tongue. Cover and cook in the oven for 1 hour or until cooked.

PASTA

SPAGHETTI WITH BUTTON ONIONS AND PEAS
Serves 4

4 oz (110 g) butter
3 rashers lean unsmoked bacon, chopped
12 button or pickling onions
1 tsp tomato purée
8 oz (225 g) cooked peas
salt and freshly ground black pepper
1 lb (450 g) spaghetti
1 tbsp chopped fresh parsley

Melt half the butter in a frying pan and add the bacon. Cover and cook over low heat for 4 minutes. Add the onions with a little water and top up the water from time to time to allow them to cook without frying. Dilute the tomato purée with a little hot water and add to the onions. Add the peas and salt and pepper to taste. Cook for 15 minutes until onions are cooked, but remain firm. Cook the spaghetti in boiling water until just soft, drain well and place in a warm serving dish. Gradually add small dots of the remaining butter to the spaghetti, mixing well. Pour the sauce over the top, sprinkle with parsley and serve at once.

NOODLES WITH MOZZARELLA CHEESE
Serves 4

4 tbsp olive oil
3 tomatoes, peeled and chopped
4 oz (110 g) Mozzarella cheese, cubed
2 oz (50 g) Cheddar cheese, grated
chopped fresh oregano
salt and freshly ground black pepper
12 oz (350 g) noodles

Heat the oil in a saucepan and add the tomatoes, Mozzarella, Cheddar and oregano; season to taste. Cover and simmer for 5 minutes or until cheese has melted. Meanwhile cook the noodles in boiling salted water, drain and place in a warm dish. Combine with the cheese mixture and serve.

NOODLES WITH CRISPY BACON
Serves 4

1 lb (450 g) fettuccine
4–5 rashers bacon
2 egg yolks
2 tbsp chopped fresh chives
8 fl oz (250 ml) cream
salt and freshly ground black pepper
1 clove garlic, crushed
grated Parmesan cheese

Cook the noodles in boiling salted water until just tender. Fry the bacon until crisp and break into pieces. Place the egg yolks, chives and cream in a bowl and mix well. Add the bacon with salt and pepper to taste. Place the mixture in a double boiler and heat until thick enough to coat a spoon. Stir in the garlic. Drain the noodles and place in a warm serving dish. Mix in the bacon mixture, tossing until the noodles are well coated. Serve with Parmesan cheese.

SPAGHETTI BOLOGNESE
Serves 4

1 oz (25 g) butter
1 onion, finely chopped
8 oz (225 g) lean beef mince
1 clove garlic, crushed
4 tomatoes, skinned and diced or 1 medium can plum tomatoes
1–2 tsp tomato purée
salt and freshly ground black pepper
¼ pt (150 ml) stock
½ oz (10 g) plain flour, blended with a little water
1 lb (450 g) spaghetti
1 tbsp olive oil
Parmesan cheese, grated

Melt the butter in a frying pan, and cook the onion until soft. Stir in the meat, garlic, tomatoes, tomato purée, salt, pepper and stock. Cover and simmer over a low heat for 40 minutes until the meat is tender, stirring occasionally. Stir in the blended flour and water. In the meantime, fill a large saucepan with water, add a dash of oil and 1 teaspoon salt. Add the spaghetti and cook for 10 minutes until just soft. Drain thoroughly, arrange on a warm serving dish and pour over the meat sauce. Sprinkle with grated Parmesan cheese and serve.

TAGLIATELLE WITH TUNA
Serves 4

12 oz (350 g) tagliatelle
1 tbsp olive oil
1 tsp salt
1 x 7 oz (200 g) can tuna fish in oil
1 medium onion, finely chopped
4 oz (110 g) mushrooms, sliced
salt and freshly ground black pepper
¼ pt (150 ml) double cream

Cook the tagliatelle until just tender in a large saucepan of boiling salted water with a dash of oil added. In the meantime, drain the oil from the tuna fish into a small saucepan. Add the onion and cook until soft, then add the mushrooms and cook until soft. Add salt and pepper to taste. Thoroughly drain the tagliatelle and return to the saucepan. Stir in the tuna, onion and mushrooms. Pour in the cream, mix well and cook gently over low heat for a few minutes. Adjust seasoning as required, arrange in a warmed bowl and serve immediately.

CHEESE AND NOODLE BAKE
Serves 4–6

1 pt (600 ml) homemade tomato sauce (see page 100)
1 lb (450 g) fettuccine
2 oz (50 g) grated Parmesan cheese
2 oz (50 g) Bel Paese cheese, diced
3 sausages, cooked and sliced
salt and freshly ground black pepper
1 tbsp butter
2 tbsp breadcrumbs
chopped fresh parsley

Preheat the oven to 350°F/180°C/Gas Mk 4. Make the tomato sauce as directed on page 100. Boil the noodles in boiling salted water with a dash of oil added for about 10 minutes or until *al dente*. Drain well and mix with the grated and diced cheeses and sliced sausages. Season well to taste and stir in the tomato sauce, mixing well but reserving ¼ pt (150 ml). Butter an ovenproof dish, sprinkle with breadcrumbs and pour the mixture in. Spoon the reserved tomato sauce over the top, sprinkle with chopped parsley and bake in the oven for 20 minutes.

SPINACH LASAGNE
Serves 4

2 oz (50 g) butter
12 oz (350 g) spinach, cooked, drained and chopped
1 oz (25 g) raisins
1 oz (25 g) pine nuts
salt and freshly ground black pepper
pinch grated nutmeg
¾ pt (450 ml) Béchamel sauce
6 oz (175 g) lasagne verde
4 oz (110 g) Cheddar cheese, grated

Preheat the oven to 375°F/190°C/Gas Mk 5. Heat the butter in a pan, add the spinach, raisins and pine nuts and cook for 2 minutes. Season with salt, pepper and nutmeg and mix in a little Béchamel sauce. Oil or grease an ovenproof dish and pour in a little Béchamel sauce, then arrange a layer of lasagne on top. Top with a layer of the spinach mixture, cover with a little more sauce and arrange another layer of lasagne on top. Top with more Béchamel and grated cheese. Repeat until all the lasagne is used up. Finish with Béchamel sauce, sprinkle with grated cheese and bake in the oven for 30 minutes.

MACARONI CHEESE WITH MUSHROOMS
Serves 4

6 oz (175 g) short-cut macaroni
2 oz (50 g) margarine
1 small onion, chopped
4 oz (110 g) mushrooms, sliced
2 oz (50 g) plain flour
1½ pt (900 ml) milk
salt and freshly ground black pepper
3 oz (75 g) Cheddar cheese, grated

Preheat the oven to 425°F/220°C/Gas Mk 7. Cook the macaroni in boiling salted water and drain well. Melt the margarine in a saucepan, add the onion and cook for 10 minutes until browned. Add the mushrooms and cook gently for a few minutes. Stir in the flour and cook for 1 minute. Gradually pour in the milk, stirring constantly. Bring to the boil, stirring, until the mixture has thickened. Add salt and pepper to taste, then stir in the cooked macaroni. Pile the mixture into a lightly greased 2½ pt (1.4 L) ovenproof dish and sprinkle over the cheese. Cook in the oven until the sauce is bubbling and the cheese has melted. Serve immediately.

PASTA BOWS WITH COURGETTES
Serves 4

3 tbsp olive oil
1 onion, finely chopped
3 tsp chopped fresh basil
4 medium courgettes, sliced
salt and white pepper
3 tomatoes, peeled and chopped
14 oz (400 g) pasta bows (farfalle)
2 oz (50 g) grated Parmesan cheese

Heat the oil in a frying pan and lightly sauté the onion and basil. Add the courgettes, season with salt and pepper and cook over a low heat for a few minutes. Add the tomatoes, cover and cook over a low heat for 30 minutes. Cook the pasta bows in boiling salted water, drain and place in a heated serving dish. Pour over the sauce, sprinkle with the cheese and serve immediately.

MACARONI AND EGG CASSEROLE
Serves 4

4½ oz (120 g) macaroni
3 pt (1.7 L) boiling water
salt and freshly ground black pepper
4 tbsp oil
1¼ oz (30 g) plain flour
1 pt (600 ml) milk
2 oz (50 g) onion, minced
2 tsp dry mustard powder
3 oz (75 g) Cheddar cheese, grated
8 oz (225 g) French beans, cooked
3–4 hard-boiled eggs, sliced

Preheat the oven to 350°F/180°C/Gas Mk 4. Add the macaroni to a large pan of salted boiling water with a dash of oil added. Cook, then drain and rinse with fresh boiling water. In the meantime, blend the oil and flour together over low heat in a small saucepan, stir in the milk and cook until thick. Stir in the onion and mustard, and season to taste with pepper and salt. Remove from the heat and add 2 oz (50 g) of the cheese. Arrange the macaroni, beans and eggs in layers in an ovenproof dish. Pour over the sauce and sprinkle over the remaining cheese. Cover and bake in the oven for 30 minutes. Remove the cover and continue to bake until the top has browned.

SPAGHETTI WITH PESTO
Serves 4

1 oz (25 g) basil leaves
2 garlic cloves, roughly chopped
pinch salt
2 oz (50 g) goat cheese, finely chopped
1½ oz (35 g) grated Parmesan cheese
4 fl oz (125 ml) oil
14 oz (400 g) spaghetti

Pound together the basil, garlic and salt with a pestle and mortar
(or use a food processor). Gradually add half the goat cheese and all
the Parmesan and mash together well. Gradually add the oil, stirring
constantly. Cook the spaghetti in boiling salted water, drain and
sprinkle with the remaining goat cheese. Stir in the basil sauce and
serve immediately.

PASTA IN LEEK AND MUSHROOM SAUCE
Serves 3

8 oz (225 g) pasta shells
1½ oz (35 g) margarine
2 leeks, trimmed and sliced
6 oz (175 g) mushrooms, sliced
1 oz (25 g) plain flour
½ pt (300 ml) chicken stock
¼ pt (150 ml) milk
salt and freshly ground black pepper
4 oz (110 g) mature Cheddar cheese

Preheat the oven to 375°F/190°C/Gas Mk 5. Cook the pasta as
directed on the packet. Drain and rinse well under cold water. Melt
the margarine in a saucepan, add the leeks and fry for 10 minutes until
tender. Stir in the mushrooms and cook for a further few minutes.
Gradually stir in the flour and cook for 1 minute, then slowly pour in
the stock and milk. Bring to the boil, and cook, stirring until the
mixture has thickened. Remove from the heat, stir in the cooked pasta
and add salt and pepper to taste. Pile the mixture into a 2 pint (1.2 L)
ovenproof dish and sprinkle the Cheddar cheese over the top. Cook
in the oven for 15–20 minutes until the cheese has melted and the
pasta is warmed through.

TAGLIATELLE WITH MUSHROOMS
Serves 4

3 tbsp olive oil
1 lb (450 g) mushrooms, sliced
juice of 1 lemon
2 tbsp chopped fresh parsley
salt
1 lb (450 g) tagliatelle

Heat the oil in a large saucepan, add the mushrooms, lemon juice, parsley and salt and cook over a low heat for 15 minutes. Cook the tagliatelle in boiling salted water, drain and set aside. Add the pasta to the sauce, mix well and heat for a few more minutes.

MACARONI CALIFORNIA
Serves 5–6

1 lb (450 g) macaroni, cooked for 5 minutes and drained
1 oz (25 g) butter, softened
8 oz (225 g) Cheddar cheese, diced
pinch salt
pinch mustard powder
2 eggs, beaten
8 fl oz (250 ml) milk
¼ pt (150 ml) single cream
¼ pt (150 ml) dry white wine
3 tbsp chopped green pepper
2 oz (50 g) breadcrumbs
1 oz (25 g) butter, melted

Preheat the oven to 325°F/170°C/Gas Mk 3. Butter an ovenproof dish. Mix together all the ingredients except for the breadcrumbs and melted butter, and put the mixture into the dish. Mix the breadcrumbs with the melted butter and sprinkle over the macaroni. Cover with foil and bake in the oven for 45–50 minutes. Remove the cover, turn off the heat, and leave for 10 minutes in the oven before serving. The top may be browned under a hot grill, but take care not to burn it.

KITCHEN GARDEN SPAGHETTI
Serves 4

4 tbsp olive oil
2 carrots, finely chopped
2 leeks, finely chopped
1 celery stalk, finely chopped
salt and freshly ground black pepper
1 oz (25 g) butter
12 oz (350 g) spaghetti
3 oz (75 g) Gruyère cheese, grated

Heat the oil in a frying pan, add all the vegetables and cook, stirring for 2 minutes. Season with salt and pepper, cover and cook slowly for 30 minutes, adding a little water to prevent sticking, if necessary. Cook the spaghetti in boiling salted water, drain and place in a saucepan with the butter. Mix well. Add the fried vegetables and the cheese and serve.

MACARONI BAKE
Serves 6–8

3 eggs
14 oz (400 g) Cheddar cheese, grated
¾ pt (450 ml) Béchamel sauce
1½ lb (675 g) lean beef mince, browned in a frying pan
9 oz (250 g) macaroni
salt and freshly ground black pepper
chopped fresh parsley

Preheat the oven to 350°F/180°C/Gas Mk 4. Beat the eggs and 4 heaped tbsp of the cheese into the Béchamel sauce. Mix 3 tbsp of this mixture into the mince. Cook the macaroni in boiling salted water until *al dente*, drain and cool slightly. Butter an ovenproof casserole and put in half the macaroni. Sprinkle with 3 tbsp cheese. Spread the mince over. Then put the rest of the macaroni on top sprinkled with more cheese and pour over the sauce. Sprinkle cheese on top of the sauce and bake for about 45 minutes or until golden brown on top. Serve with a green salad.

RIGATONI WITH MINCE
Serves 4

1 pt (600 ml) tomato sauce (see page 100)
1 lb (450 g) rigatoni or cannelloni
1 tbsp finely chopped onion
1 garlic clove, finely chopped
2 tbsp oil
12 oz (350 g) lean minced beef
2 oz (50 g) Mozzarella cheese
3 oz (75 g) Mortadella sausage
2 oz (50 g) Cheddar cheese, grated
salt and freshly ground black pepper

Make the tomato sauce as directed on page 100. Cook the rigatoni in plenty of boiling salted water with a dash of oil until *al dente*. Drain and cool. Fry the onion and garlic in the oil for about 2 minutes or until softened. Add the mince and stir until browned all over. Chop the cheese and Mortadella sausage and add to the beef. Stir well. Remove from the heat, season well, and then leave to cool. Preheat the oven to 350°F/180°C/Gas Mk 4. Fill the rigatoni by using a forcing bag, or split them, fill each half with the mince and put back together again. Arrange the stuffed rigatoni in layers in a buttered ovenproof dish, spooning a little tomato sauce and grated cheese between each layer, and finishing with a layer of tomato sauce and cheese. Bake in the oven for 20 minutes. Serve hot.

EGGS AND CHEESE

AVOCADO AND CHEESE MOUSSE
Serves 4

1 large ripe avocado
3 oz (75 g) soft cream cheese
1 garlic clove, crushed
juice of 1 lemon
salt and freshly ground black pepper
2 tbsp single cream
watercress sprigs, to garnish

Halve the avocado, remove the stone and scoop out the flesh into a
bowl. Add the cream cheese, garlic and lemon juice and mash well.
Season to taste and stir in the cream. Spoon into individual dishes and
chill for about 2 hours before serving. Serve garnished with
watercress.

VEGETABLE BAKE
Serves 6

1 oz (25 g) butter
1 oz (25 g) plain flour
1 pt (600 ml) milk
salt and freshly ground black pepper
pinch grated nutmeg
1 lb (450 g) onions, thinly sliced
2 lb (900 g) potatoes, peeled and thinly sliced
6 oz (175 g) mushrooms, sliced
1 celery stalk, chopped
¼ pt (150 ml) fresh single cream
2 oz (50 g) Cheddar cheese, grated

Preheat the oven to 350°F/180°C/Gas Mk 4. Melt the butter in a
saucepan and stir in the flour. Cook gently for 1 minute and then
gradually add the milk, whisking all the time until the sauce starts to
thicken, then add salt, pepper and nutmeg to taste. Layer the
vegetables in a shallow, buttered 2 pint (1.2 L) ovenproof dish
spreading the sauce between each layer. Pour over the cream and bake
in a preheated oven for 1 hour. Remove from the oven and scatter the
grated cheese over the top. Return to the oven for another 15 minutes
until the top is crispy and golden.

TUNA CHEESE BAKE
Serves 4

6 slices of brown bread
7 oz (200 g) can tuna in oil, drained and flaked
8 oz (225 g) mature Cheddar cheese, grated
3 eggs
1 pt (600 ml) milk
few drops of Worcester sauce
salt and freshly ground black pepper

Preheat the oven to 350°F/180°C/Gas Mk 4. Cut the bread into
cubes. Layer the bread, tuna and grated cheese in a buttered
ovenproof dish. Put the eggs, milk and Worcester sauce in a bowl and
beat together, adding salt and pepper to taste. Pour the mixture into
the dish and leave to stand for 30 minutes. Cook in the oven for
1–1¼ hours until set and golden brown. Serve hot.

EGGS PROVENÇAL
Serves 6

2 tbsp oil
2 lb (900 g) tomatoes, peeled and sliced
1 onion, chopped
1 garlic clove, crushed
1 bay leaf
2 tsp chopped fresh marjoram
2 tbsp tomato purée
pinch caster sugar
salt and freshly ground black pepper
6 eggs
chopped fresh parsley, to garnish

Preheat the oven to 350°F/180°C/Gas Mk 4. Heat the oil in a
saucepan and sauté the tomatoes, onion and garlic together for
2–3 minutes. Add the bay leaf, marjoram, tomato purée, sugar and
seasoning to taste. Cover and simmer for 30 minutes, stirring
occasionally, until the mixture has reduced to a thick purée. Remove
and discard the bay leaf. Spoon the mixture into six individual
ovenproof dishes and place on a baking sheet. Make a hollow in the
centre of each dish and carefully break an egg into each. Season lightly
and cook in the oven for 10 minutes until the eggs are set. Sprinkle
with parsley and serve immediately.

CHEESY SCOTCH EGGS
Serves 4

8 oz (225 g) pork sausage meat
4 eggs, hard-boiled
plain flour for coating
1 egg, lightly beaten
2 oz (50 g) dried breadcrumbs
1 oz (25 g) Cheddar cheese, finely grated
oil for deep frying

Divide the sausage meat into four equal-sized pieces and shape each one in an oval. Shell the eggs and roll in the flour. Using floured hands, mould a portion of sausage meat around each egg, and press the edges firmly together. Mix the breadcrumbs and cheese together. Dip the sausage-coated eggs in the beaten egg, then in the breadcrumb and cheese mixture, pressing the coating on firmly. Heat the oil in a fryer to moderate heat and fry the eggs for about 5 minutes or until golden brown. Remove and drain on absorbent kitchen paper and leave to cool.

CHEESE SOUFFLÉ
Serves 4

2 oz (50 g) butter
2 oz (50 g) plain flour
salt and freshly ground black pepper
½ pt (300 ml) milk
1 tsp made mustard
3 oz (75 g) Cheddar cheese, finely grated
3 eggs, separated

Preheat the oven to 400°F/200°C/Gas Mk 6. Melt the butter in a saucepan, add the flour and cook stirring continuously for a few minutes making sure the mixture does not turn brown. Season to taste, then gradually stir in the milk. Bring to the boil, remove from the heat and stir in the mustard and cheese. Cook for a few minutes until the cheese has melted. Leave to cool slightly, stir in the egg yolks and leave until just warm. Whisk the egg whites until stiff, stir a little of the egg white into the sauce, then carefully fold in the rest. Place in a greased 7 inch (18 cm) soufflé dish and bake in the oven for 30 minutes until well risen and golden brown.

CURRIED EGGS
Serves 4–6

2 tbsp oil
2 onions, sliced
pinch chilli powder
2 tsp curry powder
1 tbsp plain flour
¾ pt (450 ml) chicken stock
¼ pt (150 ml) malt vinegar
1 bay leaf
salt and freshly ground black pepper
1 tsp curry paste
8 eggs, hard-boiled, halved lengthwise

Heat the oil in a heavy-based saucepan and sauté the onions for
5 minutes until soft. Stir in the chilli powder, curry powder and flour
and cook, stirring continuously, for 2–3 minutes. Gradually add the
stock and vinegar and bring to the boil. Lower the heat and add the
bay leaf and salt and pepper to taste. Cover and simmer for 1 hour,
stirring occasionally. Stir in the curry paste. Add the eggs to the
mixture. Heat through, then serve in a warm serving dish lined with
boiled rice.

CHEESY AUBERGINE LAYER BAKE
Serves 4

4 medium aubergines
salt and freshly ground black pepper
2 tbsp oil
8 oz (225 g) Cheddar cheese, grated
14 oz (400 g) can tomatoes
2 tbsp fresh white breadcrumbs
1 garlic clove, crushed

Preheat the oven to 400°F/200°C/Gas Mk 6. Slice the aubergines,
place in a colander and sprinkle with salt. Leave aside for 1 hour.
Rinse the aubergines under cold running water then pat dry. Heat the
oil in a frying pan, sauté the aubergine slices a few at a time, for 2–3
minutes on each side and drain on absorbent kitchen paper. Arrange
the aubergines and grated cheese in layers in a greased ovenproof dish,
seasoning each layer with salt and pepper and ending with a layer of
cheese. Pour over the tomatoes and top with breadcrumbs mixed with
the garlic. Cook in the oven for 40 minutes and serve immediately.

CHEESE AND POTATO BAKE
Serves 6

2 oz (50 g) butter
2 lb (1 kg) old potatoes, peeled and sliced
1 lb (450 g) onions, sliced
6 oz (175 g) Cheddar cheese, grated
salt and freshly ground black pepper
chopped fresh parsley, to garnish

Preheat the oven to 350°F/180°C/Gas Mk 4. Melt the butter in an ovenproof dish, tilting the dish to coat the base and sides with butter. Arrange the potatoes, onions and cheese in layers in the dish, seasoning each layer with salt and pepper to taste and topping with a generous layer of grated cheese. Cover and cook in the oven for 1 hour, removing the lid for the last 15 minutes of cooking time. Sprinkle with parsley.

ARTICHOKE EGGS
Serves 4

4 medium globe artichokes, cooked and cooled
4 eggs, hard-boiled
½ tsp salt
¼ tsp freshly ground black pepper
¼ tsp cayenne pepper
4 oz (110 g) canned sweetcorn, drained
2 tbsp chopped fresh chives
2 tbsp double cream
1 oz (25 g) butter, melted
3 oz (75 g) Parmesan cheese, grated

Preheat the oven to 350°F/180°C/Gas Mk 4. Pull the leaves of the artichokes apart and remove the inner core. Using a spoon, scrape out the feathers in the middle of each artichoke and discard. Trim the base so that each artichoke stands upright. Place them in a baking dish. Slice the eggs in half and scoop out the yolks. Push the yolks through a sieve into a bowl. Finely chop the egg whites and add to the yolks. Mix in the salt, pepper, cayenne, sweetcorn, chives and cream. Fill the centre of each artichoke with the egg mixture and coat the leaves of the artichoke with melted butter. Sprinkle Parmesan cheese on top of each. Pour a little water around the artichokes, place the dish in the oven and bake for 10 minutes or until the filling is melted and golden brown. Serve immediately.

CHEESE AND POTATO PASTIES
Serves 4

8 oz (225 g) plain flour, sifted
pinch of salt
4 oz (110 g) lard, diced
2–3 tbsp cold water

Filling:
2 medium potatoes, chopped
1 tsp grated onion
4 oz (110 g) Cheddar cheese, diced
salt and freshly ground black pepper

Put the flour and salt in a bowl. Rub in the lard until the mixture resembles fine breadcrumbs. Mix with sufficient water to form a smooth dough. Knead into a ball, wrap in foil and chill in the refrigerator for about half an hour. Preheat the oven to 400°F/200°C/Gas Mk 6. On a floured surface, roll out the pastry and cut into four equal rounds. Place all the filling ingredients in a bowl and mix well. Put an equal amount of this mixture into each round of pastry, leaving a border around the edges. Brush the edges with water and draw the sides together. Pinch the top of the pasty together to ensure that the filling is well sealed in. Arrange the pasties on a greased baking sheet and bake in the oven for 30 minutes until golden. Serve hot or cold.

SPICY VEGETABLE PASTIES
Serves 4

8 oz (225 g) plain flour, sifted
pinch of salt
4 oz (110 g) lard, diced
2–3 tbsp cold water

Filling:
1 cooked potato, diced
2 tbsp sweetcorn
1 tbsp frozen peas, thawed
4 spring onions, finely chopped
2 hard-boiled eggs, chopped
1 tbsp curry pickle or sauce
2 oz (50 g) grated cheese seasoning

Follow method as above.

EASY PAN-BAKED PIZZA
Serves 4

1 packet pizza base
salt and freshly ground black pepper
4 medium tomatoes, thinly sliced
6 oz (175 g) Mozzarella cheese, grated
2 tsp dried oregano
1 tbsp oil

Mix together the pizza base as directed. Continue kneading until smooth and soft, then divide into two equal pieces, roll out into thin rounds and arrange on baking sheets. Preheat the oven to 425°F/220°C/Gas Mk 7. Cover each pizza base with half the tomatoes, then half the cheese. Sprinkle with oregano and season well. Sprinkle each with olive oil and cook for about 15–20 minutes.

EGGS IN BAKED POTATOES
Serves 4

4 large potatoes
1 tbsp butter
1 tbsp chopped fresh chives
1 tsp salt
¼ tsp freshly ground black pepper
¼ tsp grated nutmeg
4 tbsp double cream
4 eggs

Preheat the oven to 375°F/190°C/Gas Mk 5. Prick the potatoes with a fork. Place on the centre shelf of the oven and cook for 1½ hours. (Alternatively cook in the microwave for 25 minutes and reduce oven time.) Remove the potatoes and cut a 1 inch (2.5 cm) round from the top of each. Scoop out the potato flesh and place in a bowl, making sure not to break the potato skins. Add the butter to the bowl and mash well. Add the chives, salt, pepper and nutmeg, then stir in the cream and beat until thoroughly mixed. Gradually beat in the eggs. Divide the potato filling equally between the potato skins. Place the potatoes on a baking tray and bake in the oven for 15 minutes until the filling is lightly browned. Serve immediately.

CHEESE CUTLETS WITH SEMOLINA
Serves 4

1 pt (600 ml) milk
4 oz (110 g) semolina
4 oz (110 g) Cheddar cheese, grated
2 eggs, beaten
salt and freshly ground black pepper
cayenne pepper
a little made mustard
breadcrumbs

Boil the milk in a saucepan and sprinkle in the semolina. Continue boiling and stirring until the mixture is thick. Remove from the heat and add the cheese and seasonings. Leave to cool for a few minutes, then add one beaten egg. Return to the heat and stir until the egg is cooked, but do not boil. Place the mixture in a roasting tin which has been rinsed in cold water and left damp. When the mixture is cold, turn it out of the tin onto a floured surface. Cut into squares, sprinkle with flour and coat with the other beaten egg and breadcrumbs. Fry in very hot fat until crisp and golden. Drain on absorbent kitchen paper.

CAULIFLOWER CHEESE
Serves 4

1 cauliflower, trimmed
1½ oz (35 g) butter
3 tbsp plain flour
½ pt (300 ml) milk
4 oz (110 g) Cheddar cheese, grated
salt and freshly ground black pepper

Cook the cauliflower in boiling water until just tender. Drain and place in an ovenproof dish. Melt the butter in a saucepan, stir in the flour and cook gently for 1 minute. Remove the pan from the heat and gradually stir in the milk. Return the pan to the heat and bring to the boil, stirring until the sauce thickens. Add 3 oz (75 g) of the cheese and salt and pepper to taste. Pour the sauce over the cauliflower, sprinkle with the remaining cheese and place under a hot grill to brown.

QUICKIE SCONE PIZZA
Serves 4

8 oz (225 g) self-raising flour
½ tsp salt
2 oz (50 g) butter
¼ pt (150 ml) milk
1 large onion, thinly sliced
3 large tomatoes, peeled and thinly sliced
salt and freshly ground black pepper
½ tsp dried mixed herbs
2 oz (50 g) canned tuna fish
4 oz (110 g) Cheddar cheese, grated
oil for frying

Preheat the oven to 425°F/220°C/Gas Mk 7. Sift the flour and salt into a large bowl and rub in the butter until the mixture resembles fine breadcrumbs. Add the milk and mix to form a soft dough. Turn onto a floured surface and knead until smooth. Roll out to one large or four individual circles about ½ inch (1 cm) thick and place on a greased baking tray. Fry the onions in a little oil and use to cover the base of the pizza. Top with the tomato slices, seasoning, herbs and tuna. Finish by sprinkling the top with cheese and bake in the oven for about 20–25 minutes.

SCOTCH EGGS
Serves 4

4 eggs, hard-boiled
seasoned flour
8 oz (225 g) sausage meat
2 tsp Worcester sauce
1 egg, beaten
breadcrumbs
oil for deep frying

Dust the eggs with the seasoned flour. Mix the sausage meat with some Worcester sauce to taste and divide the mixture into four portions. Shape the sausage meat around each egg. Dip each one in the beaten egg, then roll in the breadcrumbs. Deep fry until the eggs are golden brown. Remove from the heat and drain well on greaseproof paper. Serve hot or cold.

CRUNCHY POTATOES
Serves 4

1 lb (450 g) potatoes
3 oz (75 g) butter
2 tbsp oil
2 onions, sliced
4 thick slices of bread, cubed
4 oz (110 g) Lancashire cheese, grated
salt and freshly ground black pepper
chopped fresh parsley, to garnish

Peel the potatoes, cut into small cubes and cook in boiling salted water until just tender. Drain well. Heat the butter and oil in a frying pan and fry the onions for 10–15 minutes until brown and soft. Remove from the pan and put aside. Fry the bread cubes in the pan until golden. Place the potatoes and onions back into the pan with the bread cubes and toss over a low heat for 2–3 minutes. Stir in the cheese and cook for a few minutes until the cheese melts. Add salt and pepper to taste and transfer the mixture to a warmed serving dish. Sprinkle with parsley and serve immediately.

QUICHE LORRAINE
Serves 4

6 oz (175 g) shortcrust pastry
6 oz (175 g) streaky bacon, derinded and chopped
2 eggs
2 egg yolks
¼ pt (150 ml) single cream
¼ pt (150 ml) milk
2 oz (50 g) Gruyère cheese, grated
salt and freshly ground black pepper

Preheat the oven to 375°F/190°C/Gas Mk 5. Roll out the pastry and use to line an 8 inch (20 cm) flan tin or ring. Line with greaseproof and baking beans and bake blind for 15 minutes. Remove from the oven after 20 minutes and take out the beans. Lower the heat to 350°F/180°C/Gas Mk 4. Sauté the bacon gently in its own fat until brown, drain on kitchen paper and put into the prepared flan case. Beat together the egg yolks, eggs, cream and milk, and season to taste. Pour into the prepared flan case and sprinkle with the cheese. Bake for 25–30 minutes until set and golden. Serve hot or cold.

PAN HAGGERTY
Serves 4

2 lb (900 g) Desirée potatoes, peeled
1 lb (450 g) onions
2 tbsp oil
4 oz (110 g) Cheddar cheese, grated
salt and freshly ground black pepper

Slice the onions and potatoes as thinly as possible (use the slicer on a
food processor if possible) and place in a well oiled frying pan in
layers with the cheese and seasoning. Fry very gently for 15 minutes,
when a brown crust will start to form on the base of the mixture.
Turn over with two fish slices, being careful not to break it up, and
cook for a further 15 minutes or until the potatoes are tender and the
other side of the pancake is crisp and brown. Serve cut into quarters.

CHEESE AND ONION PIE
Serves 4–6

8 oz (225 g) plain flour, sifted
salt and freshly ground black pepper
pinch dry mustard powder
3 oz (75 g) butter
4 oz (110 g) Cheddar cheese, grated

Filling:
2 oz (50 g) butter
4 large onions, sliced
6 oz (175 g) Cheddar cheese, grated
salt and freshly ground black pepper
2 tsp Worcester sauce

Preheat the oven to 375°F/190°C/Gas Mk 5. Mix together the flour,
salt, pepper and mustard in a bowl. Rub in the butter and mix in the
cheese. Use sufficient cold water to make a firm dough. Divide the
mixture in half and roll out each half on a floured surface to form two
rounds to fit an 8 inch (20 cm) pie dish. Lay one round in the pie dish
and prick the bottom with a fork. For the filling: melt the butter in a
frying pan and fry the onions until soft. Put a layer of cheese in the
pie dish, then a layer of onions and finish with a layer of cheese on
top. Season each layer. Sprinkle over the Worcester sauce and cover
with the second round of pastry. Seal the edges well and make a hole
in the centre of the pastry. Brush the top with a little milk. Bake for
35 minutes until crisp and golden brown.

CHEESE BALLS IN TOMATO SAUCE
Serves 4

8 oz (225 g) mashed potatoes
4 oz (110 g) Cheddar cheese, grated
2 tbsp chopped fresh parsley
2 oz (50 g) plain flour
1 egg, lightly beaten
breadcrumbs
oil for deep frying

Tomato sauce:
2 oz (50 g) butter
1 large onion, finely chopped
2 tbsp plain flour
4 tbsp tomato purée
½ pt (300 ml) chicken stock
1 lb (450 g) tomatoes, peeled and roughly chopped (or canned tomatoes)

Mix the potatoes with the cheese and parsley, season well and roll
into balls the size of a walnut. Lightly roll in the flour, then coat with
the egg followed by the breadcrumbs. Chill thoroughly. To make the
tomato sauce: melt the butter in a saucepan, add the onion and cook
until soft but not browned. Add the flour and cook, stirring
continuously, for a few minutes. Gradually stir in the tomato purée
and stock, bring to the boil, cover and then simmer for 15 minutes.
Season to taste, stir in the tomatoes and cook for 2 minutes. Heat the
oil and deep fry the cheese balls until golden brown then drain on
absorbent kitchen paper. Place the cheese balls on a serving dish and
serve with the sauce.

ONION QUICHE
Serves 4

6 oz (175 g) shortcrust pastry
1½ lb (675 g) large onions, thinly sliced
1½ oz (35 g) butter
3 eggs
8 fl oz (250 ml) milk
salt and freshly ground black pepper

Preheat the oven to 425°F/220°C/Gas Mk 7. Prepare and bake blind an 8 inch (20 cm) flan case as in Quiche Lorraine on page 98. Melt the butter and sauté the onions very gently until they are soft but not brown. Place the eggs, milk and seasoning in a bowl and beat together. Mix in the onions and pour the mixture into the prepared flan case. Lower the temperature and bake for 20–25 minutes until the filling is set and golden. Serve hot or cold.

SALAMI QUICHE
Serves 4

6 oz (175 g) cheese pastry
4 oz (110 g) stuffed olives, thinly sliced
4 oz (110 g) salami, thinly sliced
1 lb (450 g) tomatoes
3 eggs
½ pt (300 ml) milk
¼ pt (150 ml) plain yoghurt
2 tbsp grated Parmesan cheese
salt and freshly ground black pepper

Make the pastry in the usual way, substituting 2 oz (50 g) grated Cheddar cheese for the same amount of fat. Wrap the pastry in clingfilm and chill in the refrigerator for 30 minutes. Preheat the oven to 400°F/200°C/ Gas Mk 6. Use the pastry to line an 8 inch (20 cm) flan tin or ring and bake blind for 15 minutes. Lower the oven heat to 375°F/190°C/Gas Mk 5. Put the tomatoes in boiling water for 1 minute, drain and peel off the skins. Cut the tomatoes in half and arrange them in the base of the flan case. Put the salami and olives on top. Beat the eggs, milk and yoghurt together and season to taste with salt and pepper. Pour over the salami and tomatoes, sprinkle with Parmesan and bake in the oven for 30 minutes or until the custard is set and the top is golden brown.

SAUCY SPICY EGGS
Serves 4

8 eggs
6 oz (175 g) soft cheese
1 tbsp curry paste
4 tbsp Greek yoghurt
few sprigs fresh parsley

Boil the eggs for about 8 minutes, drain and leave to cool for a few minutes before peeling off the shells. Cut the eggs in half. Put the soft cheese, curry paste and yoghurt in a small saucepan and whisk until it starts to boil. Spoon onto warmed dinner plates and place the halved eggs on top. Garnish with sprigs of fresh parsley. The spicy eggs can be served with freshly cooked rice.

HAM AND LEEK QUICHE
Serves 4

6 oz (175 g) shortcrust pastry
1 oz (25 g) butter
2 leeks, trimmed and sliced
3 oz (75 g) cooked ham, diced
2 eggs
¼ pt (150 ml) single cream
2 tbsp chopped fresh parsley
salt and freshly ground black pepper

Preheat the oven to 375°F/190°C/Gas Mk 5. Prepare and bake blind an 8 inch (20 cm) flan case as in Quiche Lorraine on page 98. Heat the butter in a pan and cook the leeks very gently until soft but not brown. Place in the flan case and cover with the chopped ham. Beat the eggs, cream, parsley and seasoning together in a bowl. Pour into the prepared flan case and bake for 35 minutes until set and golden brown. Serve hot or cold.

LEEK AND POTATO HOT POT
Serves 4

1 lb (450 g) potatoes, peeled and sliced
2 medium leeks, trimmed and sliced
1 tbsp plain flour
salt and freshly ground black pepper
1 oz (25 g) butter
½ pt (300 ml) milk
4 oz (110 g) grated cheese

Preheat the oven to 425°F/220°C/Gas Mk 7. Place a layer of potatoes
and leeks in a greased casserole dish and sprinkle with a little flour
and seasoning. Dot with butter. Continue layering until all the
ingredients are used up, finishing with potatoes. Dot with the
remaining butter and add the milk. Cover and bake for 45 minutes,
then sprinkle over the grated cheese. Cook for another 15 minutes or
until golden brown.

POTATO BAKE
Serves 4

2 lb (900 g) potatoes, boiled
2 eggs
8 oz (225 g) cottage cheese, sieved
1–2 oz (25–50 g) fresh parsley, chopped
pinch nutmeg
salt and freshly ground black pepper
2 tbsp oil
2–3 tbsp grated Cheddar cheese
2 tomatoes, sliced

Preheat the oven to 350°F/180°C/Gas Mk 4. Mash the potatoes
with the other ingredients, except the Cheddar cheese and tomatoes,
until fluffy. Place the mixture in a deep, oiled ovenproof dish.
Sprinkle with the cheese and decorate with the tomatoes. Bake for
20–30 minutes.

SPINACH AND MINCE QUICHE
Serves 6

6 oz (175 g) shortcrust pastry
8 oz (225 g) packet frozen spinach
2 tbsp double cream
1 oz (25 g) butter
2 tbsp oil
1 onion, chopped
4 oz (110 g) minced beef
6 oz (175 g) minced pork
½ beef stock cube
1 tbsp flour
2 oz (50 g) Parmesan cheese, grated
salt and freshly ground black pepper
2 medium tomatoes, sliced

Preheat the oven to 400°F/200°C/Gas Mk 6. Prepare and bake blind an 8 inch (20 cm) flan case, as for Quiche Lorraine on page 98. Meanwhile prepare the filling. Cook the frozen spinach according to the instructions on the packet. Drain and press down very well and empty into a bowl. Stir in the double cream and leave on one side. Sauté the onion in the melted butter and oil until soft. Add the well mixed beef and pork mince and cook over a gentle heat for 25 minutes, stirring from time to time. Crumble in the beef stock cube, seasoning, flour and the cheese and mix well. Continue cooking and stirring for another 5 minutes, then leave to cool. Spoon the meat mixture into the prepared flan case and spread the spinach and cream on top. Cover with foil and bake for 30 minutes. Remove the quiche from the oven and place tomato rings on the top. Dot with butter and return to the oven without the foil covering for another 10 minutes. Serve hot.

VEGETABLES

MUSHROOM BURGERS
Serves 6

8 oz (225 g) onion, very finely chopped
8 oz (225 g) open mushrooms, finely chopped
8 oz (225 g) Cheddar cheese, grated
8 oz (225 g) fresh breadcrumbs
2 tbsp chopped fresh parsley
salt and freshly ground black pepper
2 eggs, beaten
a little flour
3–4 tbsp oil

Place the onion in boiling salted water and cook for 5 minutes until tender. Drain well and place in a bowl together with the mushrooms, cheese, breadcrumbs, parsley and salt and pepper to taste. Add the eggs and mix together thoroughly. Divide the mixture into 12 equal portions and using lightly floured hands, form into burger shapes. Arrange on a flat dish, cover with cling film and chill in the refrigerator for about 6 hours. When ready to cook, heat the oil in a non-stick pan and fry the burgers for 10 minutes, turning once so that both sides are golden brown and the burgers are cooked through.

BAKED AUBERGINES AND TOMATOES
Serves 4

¾–1 lb (350–450 g) aubergines, sliced
salt and freshly ground black pepper
8 oz (225 g) tomatoes
sunflower oil
1 tbsp chopped fresh parsley

Preheat the oven to 375°F/190°C/Gas Mk 5. Cook the aubergines for 5 minutes in boiling salted water. Drain and place on kitchen paper to remove all the liquid. Skin and slice the tomatoes. Lightly oil a shallow ovenproof dish and arrange the aubergines and tomatoes in layers, seasoning with salt and pepper to taste between each layer. Sprinkle the top with parsley and cover with foil. Bake in the oven for 40 minutes until the aubergines are tender.

CRUNCHY WALNUT BURGERS
Serves 2

1 tbsp sunflower oil
1 small onion, finely chopped
4 oz (110 g) walnuts and peanuts mixed, chopped
1½ oz (35 g) rolled oats
1 egg, beaten
2 tbsp milk
salt and freshly ground black pepper
a little oil for frying

Heat the oil in a saucepan, add the onion and fry for 5 minutes until soft. Add the nuts and oats and stir well. Add the egg, milk and salt and pepper to taste. Stir thoroughly until well blended. Divide the mixture in half and using lightly floured hands, form into two large burger shapes. Chill in the refrigerator for several hours. When ready to cook, pour a little oil into a frying pan and cook the burgers for 3 minutes on each side until brown and crisp.

SPINACH AND POTATO RING
Serves 4

1 oz (25 g) butter
1½ lb (675 g) leaf spinach, rinsed, dried and chopped
salt and freshly ground black pepper
grated nutmeg
1½ lb (675 g) potatoes, cubed
4 fl oz (125 ml) milk, warmed
1 egg yolk
2 tbsp grated Parmesan cheese

Melt half the butter in a pan, stir in the spinach and gently cook for 12 minutes. Sprinkle with salt, nutmeg and pepper to taste. Cook the potatoes in boiling salted water for 15–20 minutes, until tender. Drain well, pour in the milk, remaining butter and some nutmeg. Add some salt if required. Preheat the oven to 400°F/200°C/Gas Mk 6. Mash the potatoes thoroughly and beat in the egg yolk, Parmesan cheese and spinach. Mix well until all the ingredients are thoroughly blended, pile the mixture into a greased 2 pt (1.2 L) ring mould and cook in the oven for 20 minutes until firm. To serve, loosen the edges of the mould with a knife and turn out onto a large warmed serving dish.

CABBAGE AND BACON
Serves 4

1 small white cabbage
1 tbsp sunflower oil
4 oz (110 g) bacon pieces, roughly chopped

Finely shred the cabbage removing the outer leaves. Heat the oil in a
large saucepan, and fry the bacon until the fat runs out. Increase the
heat and fry until the bacon is crisp. Stir in the cabbage and cook over
high heat for 5 minutes, continuously tossing the cabbage. Serve
immediately.

VEGETABLE CASSEROLE
Serves 4

8 small onions
salt
12 oz (350 g) small carrots
1 small swede, diced
12 oz (350 g) fresh peas, shelled, or a medium packet of frozen peas
12 oz (350 g) potatoes

Sauce:
1½ oz (35 g) margarine
1½ oz (35 g) plain flour
¾ pt (450 ml) milk
1 tsp French mustard
6 oz (175 g) Cheddar cheese, grated

Simmer the onions in salted water for 5 minutes. Add the carrots,
swede and peas and continue to cook until all the vegetables are
nearly tender. Remove from the heat and strain, reserving about ¼ pt
(150 ml) of the liquid. In the meantime, parboil the potatoes in a
saucepan of salted water until just soft. Remove from the heat and
carefully drain off the water. Slice the potatoes thickly. Preheat the
oven to 375°F/190°C/Gas Mk 5. To make the sauce, heat the
margarine in a pan, stir in the flour and cook gently for a few minutes,
stirring constantly. Remove from the heat and gradually pour in the
milk and the reserved vegetable stock, stirring all the time. Return to
the heat, bring to the boil and cook until thickened. Stir in salt and
pepper to taste, mustard and three-quarters of the cheese. Mix
together all the vegetables and sauce and pile into an ovenproof dish.
Arrange the sliced potatoes on top and sprinkle with the remaining
cheese. Bake in the oven for 20 minutes until the potatoes are golden.

SARATOGA POTATOES
Serves 4

4 firm potatoes
oil and butter for frying
salt and freshly ground black pepper
4 fl oz (125 ml) double cream (optional)

Boil the potatoes in their skins in boiling salted water. Cook them slowly, drain and leave to cool. When cold chill in the refrigerator at least overnight, but longer if possible. Do not peel off the skins at this stage. When ready to use, heat a generous amount of oil and butter together in a deepish frying pan. Peel the potatoes and cut them into small cubes. Season well with salt and pepper and fry gently for about 5 minutes, turning over with a slotted spoon. Pour in the double cream, cover the pan and cook for a further 5 minutes. Serve hot. Add chopped fresh or dried herbs, if liked.

CHEESY LEEKS WITH BACON
Serves 4

4 medium leeks
8 rashers lean bacon, lightly grilled

Sauce:
1 oz (25 g) butter
1 oz (25 g) plain flour
½ pt (300 ml) milk
3 oz (75 g) Cheddar cheese, grated
1 tsp Dijon mustard
salt and freshly ground black pepper
fresh parsley, to garnish

Preheat the oven to 350°F/180°C/Gas Mk 4. Cut off the coarse green leaves from the leeks and make a deep slit through the green and half of the white part and open up. Thoroughly wash, then wrap each leek in 2 rashers of bacon. Lay in a shallow ovenproof dish. Melt the butter in a saucepan and stir in the flour. Cook for 1 minute, then gradually pour in the milk and bring to the boil. Continue to boil, stirring constantly, until the sauce has thickened. Remove from the heat, stir in two-thirds of the cheese and the mustard and season with salt and pepper to taste. Pour over the leeks and sprinkle the remaining cheese over the top. Bake in the oven for 1 hour until leeks are tender. Garnish with parsley and serve at once.

POTATOES DAUPHINOISE
Serves 4

1 lb (450 g) medium potatoes, peeled and sliced
salt and freshly ground black pepper
pinch nutmeg
1 pt (600 ml) milk, warmed
1 egg, beaten
2 oz (50 g) butter
2 oz (50 g) Gruyère cheese, grated
1 garlic clove

Heat the oven to 325°F/177°C/Gas Mk 3. Season the potatoes with salt and pepper and nutmeg, mix well and put in a bowl. Beat the egg and strain into the warm milk. Sprinkle two-thirds of the cheese onto the potatoes and mix well. Rub a shallow ovenproof dish well with garlic and butter it. Spoon the potatoes into the dish and pour over the milk. Sprinkle the remaining cheese on top and dot with butter. Bake in a preheated oven for 30–40 minutes or until the potatoes are cooked through and the dish is golden and crispy on top.

SPINACH WITH ALMONDS
Serves 4

2 lb (900 g) leaf spinach
2 oz (50 g) butter
½ onion, finely chopped
salt
grated nutmeg
2 egg yolks
4 tbsp double cream
2 oz (50 g) flaked almonds

Thoroughly rinse and drain the spinach and tear the leaves into medium pieces. Melt the butter in a frying pan, and fry the onion for 2–3 minutes until soft. Gradually add the spinach, turning it so that the butter coats each piece. Add nutmeg and salt and pepper to taste. Cook over low heat for 10 minutes until spinach is tender. Beat the egg yolks and cream in a bowl, then add to the spinach mixture. Remove from heat and arrange on a warm serving dish. Cook the almonds in the pan in the remaining butter, stirring, until golden brown. Mix the almonds into the spinach and serve immediately.

GLAZED TURNIPS
Serves 4

1 lb (450 g) new turnips
3 oz (75 g) butter
salt
1 tsp sugar

Peel the turnips and cut into small barrel shapes. Melt half the butter and sauté the turnips. Season with salt, sprinkle with sugar and sauté for a few seconds over a high flame to brown them a little. Add enough water just to cover and simmer gently for 20 minutes until the liquid has almost disappeared. Remove from the heat, add the remaining butter and shake to glaze.

BAKED POTATOES
Serves 1

large baking potatoes
butter
soured cream
chopped fresh chives

Preheat the oven to 400°F/200°C/Gas Mk 6. Wash and dry the potatoes, rub lightly with oil and bake in the oven for about 1½ hours until soft. Cut a cross in the top of each potato, press to open and insert a good knob of butter. Add a spoonful of soured cream mixed with chives. The potatoes can be partially cooked in the microwave and then crisped in the oven, if preferred. Use any combination of toppings, including grated cheese, chopped fried bacon, chopped fresh herbs.

PEAS WITH SHALLOTS
Serves 6

1½ lb (675 g) frozen peas
2 carrots, sliced
8 oz (225 g) shallots, sliced
2 oz (50 g) ham, diced
2 tbsp butter
salt and freshly ground black pepper
chicken or vegetable stock or water

Put the peas, carrots, shallots and ham in a pan and fry in butter over a very low heat for 12 minutes. Season, add 2 tbsp stock or water and simmer until tender.

AUSTRIAN POTATOES AND CABBAGE
Serves 4

5 medium potatoes
1 medium Savoy cabbage, shredded
salt and freshly ground black pepper
2 hard-boiled eggs, sliced
2 oz (50 g) butter
¼ pt (150 ml) cream
2 tbsp breadcrumbs

Preheat the oven to 400°F/200°C/Gas Mk 6. Boil the potatoes in their skins in salted water, then peel and slice. Cook the cabbage for about 3 minutes in salted water. Drain well. Butter an ovenproof dish and arrange the potatoes, eggs and cabbage in layers, sprinkling each layer with a little melted butter, cream and salt and pepper to taste. Finish with a layer of cabbage. Sprinkle with breadcrumbs, dot with small pieces of butter and bake in the oven for 10–12 minutes until the top is browned.

CHICORY AU GRATIN
Serves 4

4–6 small heads of chicory
juice of 2 lemons
4 tbsp oil
1 tbsp chopped fresh basil
salt and freshly ground black pepper
4 tbsp double cream
5 oz (150 g) Mozzarella cheese, sliced

Preheat the oven to 425°F/220°C/Gas Mk 7. Rinse and drain the chicory. Remove the thick stems and cut the heads into rings. Sprinkle with lemon juice and leave to stand for a few minutes. Place the oil in a bowl and beat in the basil and salt and pepper to taste. Fold into the cream and pour over the chicory, stirring so that the chicory is well coated in the sauce. Arrange in an ovenproof dish, place the sliced cheese on top and cook in the oven for 15–20 minutes. Serve at once.

SWEET AND SOUR RED CABBAGE
Serves 6

12 oz (350 g) red cabbage, shredded
1 lb (450 g) Bramley apples, peeled, cored and sliced
¼ pt (150 ml) water
1½ oz (35 g) soft light brown sugar
salt
4 cloves
6 tbsp white wine vinegar
1 oz (25 g) margarine
1 tbsp redcurrant jelly

Place all the ingredients in a saucepan and bring to the boil. Lower the heat, cover and simmer for 45 minutes, stirring occasionally, until the cabbage is tender. Check seasoning and remove cloves before serving.

COURGETTES WITH PARSLEY
Serves 4

2 oz (50 g) margarine or butter
1 lb (450 g) courgettes, thinly sliced
salt and freshly ground black pepper
2 tbsp chopped fresh parsley

Heat the margarine in a frying pan, and fry the courgettes. Season with salt and pepper to taste. Fry briskly for 5 minutes until the courgettes are pale golden brown. Arrange on a warm dish, sprinkle with parsley and serve.

RED CABBAGE AND POTATO GRATIN
Serves 4

2 lb (900 g) potatoes, peeled, boiled and halved
½ oz (10 g) butter
2 oz (50 g) streaky bacon, derinded and chopped
1 small onion, chopped
12 oz (350 g) red cabbage, shredded
salt
½ tsp curry powder
pinch cayenne pepper
pinch paprika

Place the potatoes in a greased ovenproof dish. Melt the butter in a frying pan, add the bacon and onion and cook until the bacon is crisp. Remove about one-third of the mixture and set aside. Stir the cabbage into the pan with salt with taste, then add the curry powder, cayenne and paprika. Stir thoroughly and cook for 2–3 minutes. Pour over the potatoes and sprinkle the reserved bacon and onion mixture on top. Cook under a preheated grill until the top is golden brown and serve immediately.

BRAISED CELERY
Serves 6

1 head celery, strings removed
1 lb (450 g) onions, sliced
salt and freshly ground black pepper
1 pt (600 ml) chicken or vegetable stock
chopped fresh parsley

Preheat the oven to 350°F/180°C/Gas Mk 4. Cut the celery into 3 inch (7.5 cm) lengths. Arrange in layers with the onions in a 3 pint (1.8 L) ovenproof dish, seasoning each layer with salt and pepper to taste. Pour in the stock. Cover and cook in the oven for 1 hour or until the celery is tender. Sprinkle with parsley and serve.

BAKED ONIONS
Serves 4

4 medium onions
butter
salt and freshly ground black pepper
chopped fresh parsley

Preheat the oven to 350°F/180°C/Gas Mk 4. Peel the onions and leave them whole. Cut out four pieces of foil and stand an onion on each. Place a knob of butter on top of each onion and sprinkle with salt and pepper. Seal the onion inside the foil, place in an ovenproof dish and bake in the oven for about 1 hour or until the onions are tender. (The size of the onions will determine the cooking time.) Unwrap the onions, sprinkle with parsley and serve.

CREAMED SAVOY CABBAGE
Serves 4

2 lb (900 g) Savoy cabbage
1 oz (25 g) lard
1 onion, chopped
½ pt (300 ml) beef stock
pinch grated nutmeg
salt and freshly ground black pepper
¼ pt (150 ml) soured cream

Remove the thick stems from the cabbage and cut the leaves into wide strips. Wash and drain thoroughly. Melt the lard in a large saucepan, add the onion and cook for 5 minutes. Stir in the cabbage, stock and nutmeg and season to taste with salt and pepper. Cover and cook over low heat for 20 minutes, stirring from time to time. Drain off any excess liquid. Stir the soured cream into the cabbage, arrange on a warm dish and serve immediately.

STUFFED SPANISH ONIONS
Serves 4

2 large Spanish onions, halved
salt and freshly ground black pepper
1 oz (25 g) butter

Stuffing:
4 oz (110 g) smoked bacon, derinded and chopped
3 tomatoes, peeled and chopped
4 oz (110 g) button mushrooms, sliced
1 tbsp chopped fresh parsley
2 tbsp grated Parmesan cheese
1–2 tsp dried oregano

Preheat the oven to 425°F/220°C/Gas Mk 7. Scoop out a hollow in each half onion, reserving the onion pulp. Place the onion halves in a saucepan of water, add some salt and bring to the boil. Cook for 15 minutes until almost soft. Drain thoroughly. Melt half the butter in a frying pan. Chop up the reserved onion pulp and place in the pan together with the bacon. Fry for 4–5 minutes, then add the tomatoes and mushrooms and cook for 2–3 minutes. Remove from the heat, stir in the parsley, cheese, salt and pepper to taste, and the oregano. Pile the mixture into the onion halves and dot each one with the remaining butter. Place each onion half carefully in a greased ovenproof dish and bake in the oven for 12–15 minutes.

TURNIP AU GRATIN
Serves 6

1 pt (600 ml) beef stock
wine vinegar
pinch sugar
2 lb (900 g) turnips, sliced
½ oz (10 g) butter
1 tbsp plain flour
4 tbsp double cream
4 oz (110 g) Gruyère cheese, sliced

Put the stock, a dash of vinegar and the sugar in a saucepan and bring to the boil. Remove from the heat, add the turnips and bring back to the boil. Lower the heat and cook for 20 minutes. Preheat the oven to 400°F/ 200°C/Gas Mk 6. In the meantime, melt the butter in a pan, stir in the flour and cook for 2–3 minutes. Whisk in ½ pt (300 ml) of the turnip cooking liquid, blending well to make a smooth sauce. Gradually stir in the cream. Thoroughly drain the turnips and arrange in a lightly greased ovenproof dish. Pour over the sauce and arrange the cheese slices on top. Cook in the oven for 15 minutes until golden.

FENNEL WITH CHEESE SAUCE
Serves 4–6

2–3 heads fennel
juice of 1 lemon
½ pt (300 ml) beef stock
salt and freshly ground black pepper
pinch sugar
pinch ground coriander
4 oz (110 g) Emmenthal cheese, grated
¼ pt (150 ml) double cream
5 oz (150 g) cooked ham, chopped
½ oz (10 g) butter

Remove the stalks and leaves from the fennel and cut the heads into large pieces. Sprinkle over the lemon juice. Pour the stock into a shallow pan and bring to the boil. Add the fennel, sugar, coriander and salt and pepper to taste. Lower the heat and cook for 15 minutes. Mix in the cheese and cream and continue to simmer, but keep stirring until the cheese has melted. Sprinkle the ham and butter on the top and place under a hot grill for 3 minutes until the top is bubbling. Serve at once.

MEXICAN SWEETCORN
Serves 4

1 oz (25 g) butter
12 oz (350 g) can sweetcorn, drained
½ chilli pepper, deseeded and sliced
1 red pepper, deseeded and chopped
2 garlic cloves, crushed
3 tsp lemon juice
salt

Heat half the butter in a frying pan. Add the drained sweetcorn together with the chilli, red pepper and garlic. Mix together well and cook over low heat for 4–5 minutes. Pour in the lemon juice with salt to taste and the remaining butter. Stir the mixture well and serve immediately on a warm dish.

PEAS IN MINT SAUCE
Serves 4–6

¼ pt (150 ml) beef stock
1 lb (450 g) shelled fresh peas
2 tomatoes, peeled and chopped
½ oz (10 g) butter
4 fresh mint sprigs, chopped
4 tbsp double cream
salt and freshly ground black pepper

Pour the stock into a saucepan and add the peas and tomatoes. Bring to the boil, then lower the heat and cook gently for 15–20 minutes. Stir in the butter. Place the mint and cream in a bowl and mix well with a little of the cooking liquid from the peas. Remove the saucepan from heat, stir in the mint mixture and add salt and pepper to taste. Place in a warm dish and serve immediately.

MARROW IN DILL BUTTER
Serves 4

2 lb (900 g) marrow
2 oz (50 g) butter
2 onions, finely chopped
1 sprig of fresh dill, chopped
salt and freshly ground black pepper

Peel the marrow, remove the seeds and chop into cubes. Melt the butter in a large saucepan, add the onion and cook for 5 minutes. Stir in the marrow cubes and cook over low heat for 15 minutes until tender. Arrange in a warm dish, sprinkle with the dill, add salt and pepper to taste and serve immediately.

CAULIFLOWER CASSEROLE
Serves 4

1¼ pt (750 ml) beef stock
1 large cauliflower, cut into florets
pinch grated nutmeg
1 tbsp chopped fresh herbs
3 eggs
1 tbsp milk
1 tbsp grated Parmesan cheese

Preheat the oven to 400°F/200°C/Gas Mk 6. Pour the stock into a large saucepan and bring to the boil. Add the cauliflower and the nutmeg. Return to the boil, lower the heat, cover and cook gently for 10 minutes. Drain and arrange the cauliflower in a lightly greased casserole dish. Sprinkle over the herbs. In a bowl, beat together the eggs, milk and Parmesan cheese and pour over the cauliflower. Cook in the oven for 20 minutes until the egg has set.

STUFFED GREEN PEPPERS
Serves 4

4 small green peppers
6 tomatoes, peeled and chopped
1 tbsp fresh basil, chopped
salt and freshly ground black pepper
4 eggs
paprika

Preheat the oven to 425°F/220°C/Gas Mk 7. Slice the top off each pepper and remove the seeds and pith. Rinse each pepper thoroughly and leave upside-down to drain. Place the tomatoes in a bowl, and add the basil with salt and pepper to taste. Mix well and pile into each pepper. Crack a raw egg into each pepper and sprinkle the top with salt and paprika. Arrange in an ovenproof dish and cook in oven for 10–15 minutes. Serve immediately.

GRILLED ONION AND POTATO SLICES
Serves 4

2 large onions, thinly sliced
4 large potatoes, thickly sliced
salt and freshly ground black pepper
Sauce:
1 oz (25 g) margarine
1 oz (25 g) plain flour
½ pt (300 ml) milk
2–3 oz (50–75 g) Cheddar cheese, grated

Place the onions and potato slices in boiling salted water, cook until just tender and strain well. In the meantime, to make the sauce, heat the margarine in a saucepan, stir in the flour and cook for several minutes. Gradually pour in the milk, stirring, bring to the boil and cook, stirring, until thick and smooth. Add salt and pepper to taste. Arrange the onions and potatoes in layers in an ovenproof dish and pour over the sauce. Sprinkle grated cheese on top and place under a hot grill until crisp and golden brown.

BRUSSELS SPROUTS AU GRATIN
Serves 4

1½ lb (675 g) Brussels sprouts, trimmed
pinch grated nutmeg
salt
1 oz (25 g) butter
½ onion, chopped
4 oz (110 g) cooked ham, cut into strips
3 tbsp Parmesan cheese, grated

Preheat the oven to 400°F/200°C/Gas Mk 6. Pour 1 pt (600 ml) of water into a large saucepan and bring to the boil. Add the Brussels sprouts together with the nutmeg and salt to taste. Bring back to the boil, lower the heat, cover and cook gently for 10–15 minutes. Drain well and arrange in an ovenproof dish. Melt half the butter in a frying pan, add the onion and cook for 4–5 minutes. Stir in the ham. Sprinkle over the Brussels sprouts, then sprinkle with the Parmesan cheese. Dot over the remaining butter and cook in the oven for 20 minutes until the top is golden brown.

BAKED PARSNIP WITH CHEESY TOPPING
Serves 4

1 lb (450 g) parsnips, peeled
8 oz (225 g) ham, chopped
oil
8 oz (225 g) can tomatoes
1 tbsp chopped fresh parsley
salt and freshly ground black pepper
2 oz (50 g) Cheddar cheese, grated
a little Parmesan cheese
2 oz (50 g) fresh breadcrumbs

Preheat the oven to 350°F/180°C/Gas Mk 4. Remove the hard cores from the parsnips and chop. Place in a bowl, add the ham and mix well. Pile into a lightly greased 2 pint (1.2 L) ovenproof dish. Arrange the tomatoes on top, sprinkle with parsley, salt and pepper to taste. Put the Cheddar cheese and Parmesan cheese in a bowl, add the bread-crumbs, stirring well, then sprinkle over the parsnips. Bake in the oven for 45 minutes until the parsnips are tender and the top is crisp and golden brown.

MEDITERRANEAN BEAN STEW
Serves 4

1 large onion, chopped
8 oz (225 g) smoked streaky bacon, derinded and chopped
2 tbsp vegetable oil
2 celery stalks, thinly sliced
1 garlic clove, crushed
1 lb (450 g) tomatoes
2 x 15 oz (425 g) cans butter beans, drained
½ pt (300 ml) chicken stock
1 bay leaf
salt and freshly ground black pepper
chopped fresh basil

Sauté the onion and bacon in half the oil for about 5 minutes. Add the celery and garlic and cook for a further 4 minutes until soft. Put the tomatoes in a bowl and pour over boiling water. Leave for 1 minute, drain and when cool enough to handle, peel off the skins. Cut the tomatoes into quarters and add to the bacon and onion mixture together with the beans, bay leaf and stock. Season well, cover the pan and cook for 10 minutes over a gentle heat. Sprinkle with the basil and serve hot with crusty bread.

GYPSY POTATOES
Serves 4–5

4 oz (110 g) butter
1½ lb (675 g) potatoes, sliced
salt and freshly ground black pepper
1 lb (450 g) tomatoes
1 medium onion
2 oz (50 g) soft breadcrumbs

Preheat the oven to 400°F/200°C/Gas Mk 6. Melt the butter in a large saucepan. Toss the potato slices in the butter until well coated. Sprinkle with salt and pepper to taste. Place the tomatoes into boiling water for 1 minute, then immediately dip into cold water and remove the skins. Grate the onion into a bowl, add the tomatoes and mix well. Season with more salt and pepper. Place layers of the potato and the tomato and onion mixture in an ovenproof dish, finishing with a layer of potatoes on top. Sprinkle over the breadcrumbs and pour any remaining butter from the saucepan over the top. Bake in the oven for about 1¼ hours or until the potatoes are tender and the top is golden brown and crisp.

FRENCH PEAS
Serves 4

1 lb (450 g) shelled fresh peas
1 bunch spring onions, trimmed and chopped
2 oz (50 g) butter
1 tsp sugar
salt and freshly ground black pepper
4 tbsp water
1 crisp lettuce

Put the peas and spring onions in a heavy-based saucepan. Add half the butter, the sugar and salt and pepper to taste. Add the water and bring to the boil. Lower the heat, cover and simmer gently for 10 minutes. Remove and discard the outer leaves of the lettuce. Cut the lettuce heart into quarters and add to the peas and onions. Cover and simmer for 3–5 minutes, shaking the saucepan from time to time. Remove from the heat, add the remaining butter and toss thoroughly. Place in a warm dish and serve immediately.

PEAS AND ONIONS WITH YOGHURT SAUCE
Serves 4–6

1 lb (450 g) fresh shelled peas
8 oz (225 g) pickling onions, topped and tailed
1 oz (25 g) margarine
1 oz (25 g) plain flour
¼ pt (150 ml) yoghurt
salt and freshly ground black pepper

Place the peas and onions in two separate saucepans of boiling salted water and cook until just tender. Drain the water from the vegetables, reserving ½ pt (300 ml) of the onion water. Put the vegetables aside and keep warm. Melt the margarine in a saucepan, stir in the flour and cook for 1 minute. Gradually pour in the onion water, bring to the boil, stirring until thick. Remove from the heat, stir in the yoghurt and season to taste with salt and pepper. Gradually fold in the peas and onions, then transfer to a warm dish to serve.

MUSHROOM SOUFFLÉ
Serves 4

1 oz (25 g) margarine or butter
8 oz (225 g) button mushrooms, sliced
1 oz (25 g) plain flour
½ pt (300 ml) milk
4 eggs, separated
salt and freshly ground black pepper
1 tbsp chopped fresh parsley
1 oz (25 g) Cheddar cheese, grated
1 oz (25 g) fresh breadcrumbs

Preheat the oven to 375°F/190°C/Gas Mk 5. Melt the margarine in a saucepan, and fry the mushrooms for 5 minutes until soft. Stir in the flour and cook for 1 minute. Gradually pour in the milk. Bring to the boil, stirring constantly, until the sauce has thickened. Remove from the heat and stir in the egg yolks, parsley and salt and pepper to taste. Place the egg whites in a bowl and whisk until soft peaks form. Fold into the mushroom sauce until well blended and transfer to a shallow lightly greased 2 pt (1.2 L) ovenproof dish. Mix together the cheese and breadcrumbs and sprinkle over the top of the soufflé. Cook in the oven for 25 minutes until the soufflé is well risen and a golden colour. Serve immediately.

MUSHROOM SAUTÉ
Serves 6–8

2 oz (50 g) butter
2 lb (900 g) button mushrooms
1 small onion, chopped
2 tomatoes, peeled and cut into wedges
½ cucumber, chopped
salt and freshly ground black pepper
1 tbsp lemon juice
1 small bunch fresh herbs, chopped

Melt the butter in a saucepan and add the mushrooms and onion. Cook for 5 minutes over moderate heat, then reduce the heat and cook for 20 minutes until the vegetables are tender. Mix in the tomatoes and cucumber and cook for a further 3–5 minutes. Mix in the lemon juice with salt and pepper to taste. Add the herbs and serve immediately.

VEGETARIAN PAELLA
Serves 4

2 tbsp olive oil
1 onion, finely chopped
2 garlic cloves, finely chopped
2 tomatoes, finely chopped
7 oz (200 g) rice
salt
few strands of saffron
1 green pepper, deseeded and finely sliced
4 oz (110 g) peas
4 oz (110 g) broad beans
1 tbsp chopped parsley

Heat the oil in a large frying pan or paella pan. Fry the onion and garlic for 2 minutes then add the tomatoes and cook for a few more minutes. Add the rice, salt and saffron strands. Mix well and add water (approximately double the amount of the rice). Cook over low heat until the rice is tender. Towards the end of the cooking time, add the pepper, peas and broad beans. Leave to stand for a few minutes then serve garnished with parsley.

POTATO AND BACON SAVOURY
Serves 4

3 spring onions, chopped
3 eggs
½ pt (300 ml) milk
½ tsp dried sage
salt and freshly ground black pepper
1½ lb (675 g) mashed potatoes
8 oz (225 g) bacon, diced
grated cheese

Fry the onion until crisp. Place the eggs in a bowl and beat well, adding the milk, sage and onion. Season well with salt and pepper to taste. Grease an ovenproof dish and arrange the mashed potato around the edge. Use a fork to fluff up the potatoes. Place the bacon in the middle and pour the egg mixture over the top of the bacon. Sprinkle over some cheese. Bake in the oven for 30 minutes until the egg has set and the potatoes are golden brown.

POTATO RATATOUILLE
Serves 4

4 tbsp olive oil
2 large onions, sliced
2 garlic cloves, crushed
12 oz (350 g) potatoes, cubed
4 oz (110 g) courgettes, sliced
3 large tomatoes, peeled
2 green peppers, deseeded and sliced
pinch oregano
salt and freshly ground black pepper
1 tbsp finely chopped fresh parsley

Heat the oil in a deep frying pan. Cook the onions and garlic gently until the onions are transparent. Add the potatoes, courgettes, tomatoes, peppers and oregano and season with salt and pepper. Cover and simmer gently for 20 minutes or until the potatoes are cooked. If the ratatouille is too dry, add a little water. Stir in the parsley just before serving.

BROAD BEAN PURÉE
Serves 4

5 lb (2.3 kg) broad beans, in the pods
3 oz (75 g) butter
salt and freshly ground black pepper
pinch nutmeg

Shell the beans. Cook in boiling water for about 10 minutes or until very tender. Drain, reserving the cooking water. Purée with a little of the cooking water. Return to the heat and stir in the butter and seasoning. Cook over a very low heat, stirring constantly, for 5 minutes or until piping hot.

VEGETABLE PILAU
Serves 4

olive oil for frying
3 garlic cloves, crushed
4 oz (110 g) mushrooms, sliced
4 oz (110 g) courgettes, sliced
2 leeks, trimmed and sliced
2 onions, thinly sliced
1 red and 1 green pepper, deseeded and sliced
4 oz (110 g) cauliflower florets
4 oz (110 g) mangetout, trimmed
12 oz (300 g) cashew nuts or almonds
1 tbsp chopped fresh tarragon
1 lb (450 g) long-grain rice
4 oz (110 g) tomatoes, skinned and sliced
3 tbsp chopped fresh parsley or coriander
salt and freshly ground black pepper
2 tsp ground turmeric

Heat some olive oil in a very large pan and sauté the garlic, mushrooms, courgettes, leeks, onions, pepper, cauliflower and mangetout for a few minutes. Stir in the nuts, tarragon, rice, tomatoes, parsley or coriander and seasoning to taste. Cook for another minute, adding extra olive oil if the mixture looks too dry. Add 2 pints (1.2 L) of water, boil for 10 minutes, then add the turmeric. Cover tightly and simmer for 45 minutes. Once cooked turn off the heat and leave the rice to dry out for about 30 minutes. Preheat the oven to 350°F/180°C/Gas Mk 4. Transfer to an ovenproof dish and cook in the oven for 15 minutes before serving.

BEAN VEGETABLE CASSEROLE
Serves 4

2 tbsp oil
1 large onion, chopped
3 celery stalks, chopped
3 carrots, sliced
14 oz (400 g) can tomatoes
2 tbsp tomato purée
½ pt (300 ml) stock
15 oz (425 g) can red kidney beans, drained
salt and freshly ground black pepper
1 small cauliflower, separated into small florets
4 oz (110 g) button mushrooms

Heat the oil in a large saucepan and quickly fry the onion, celery and carrots until just turning brown. Add the tomatoes, purée, stock, beans and salt and pepper to taste. Cover with a lid and simmer over low heat for 20 minutes until the carrots are just tender. Add the cauliflower and mushrooms, replace the lid and cook for 5–10 minutes. Serve at once.

VEGETABLE CHOP SUEY
Serves 4

3 carrots
2 cucumbers
2 tbsp olive oil
2 onions, sliced
3 peppers, deseeded and sliced
3 courgettes, cubed
2 tomatoes, peeled and chopped
4 oz (110 g) mushrooms, sliced
1 tsp coriander
1 tsp cinnamon
1 tsp ginger
2 tbsp soy sauce

Cut the carrots and cucumbers into thick match sticks. Heat the oil in a frying pan and sauté the onions, peppers, carrots and cucumbers for 10 minutes. Add the courgettes, tomatoes and mushrooms, season with the spices, cook for 2 minutes then stir in the soy sauce and serve.

VEGETABLE CRUMBLE
Serves 4

2 lb (900 g) mixed root vegetables, chopped
2 tsp vegetable oil
1 onion, chopped
1 oz (25 g) cashew nuts
2 tbsp plain flour
¼ pt (150 ml) milk
½ pt (300 ml) vegetable stock (from above)
1 tsp dried rosemary
salt and freshly ground black pepper

Topping:
2 oz (50 g) porridge oats
2 oz (50 g) finely chopped nuts
2 tbsp vegetable oil

Preheat the oven to 375°F/190°C/Gas Mk 5. Cook the vegetables in boiling salted water until just tender. Drain, retaining the vegetable water for stock. Gently fry the onion in the oil until soft and add the cashew nuts and cook for a couple of minutes. Stir in the flour and mix to a paste with some of the milk. Slowly add the remaining milk and stock and bring to the boil, stirring all the time. Simmer until thickened. Season with salt and pepper to taste. Add the vegetables and pour into a greased ovenproof dish. Mix all the topping ingredients together to form a crumble and cover the vegetables. Place in the oven and cook for about half an hour.

HONEY CARROTS
Serves 4

1 lb (450 g) young carrots, sliced
1 oz (25 g) butter
1 tbsp runny honey
chopped fresh parsley

Place the carrots in boiling salted water and cook for 10 minutes until just tender. Drain thoroughly. Place the butter and honey in a saucepan, heat and then add the carrots. Cook for a few minutes, stirring until all the carrot slices are coated with the honey. Turn onto a warm serving dish and sprinkle with parsley.

LENTIL HOT POT
Serves 4

8 oz (225 g) red lentils, washed
1½ lb (675 g) potatoes, sliced
3 tomatoes, sliced
3 onions, sliced
salt and freshly ground black pepper
2 tsp yeast extract
¾ pt (450 ml) vegetable stock
2 oz (50 g) margarine or butter
1 tsp dried herbs
3 oz (75 g) grated cheese

Preheat the oven to 375°F/190°C/Gas Mk 5. Layer the lentils, potatoes, tomatoes and onions in an ovenproof dish, seasoning between the layers and finishing with potato. Dissolve the yeast extract in the vegetable stock and pour over. Dot with margarine, sprinkle with herbs and cover. Bake in the oven for about an hour, or until tender. Remove the lid and sprinkle grated cheese over. Put under the grill until the top is brown.

BROCCOLI AND CAULIFLOWER POLONAISE
Serves 4

12 oz (350 g) cauliflower, separated into florets
12 oz (350 g) broccoli spears
1½ oz (35 g) margarine
1 oz (25 g) fresh breadcrumbs
1 tbsp chopped fresh parsley
1 hard-boiled egg, chopped

Place the cauliflower and broccoli in boiling salted water and cook for 4 minutes so that the vegetables are still crisp in the middle. Thoroughly drain off the water and arrange the vegetables on a warm serving dish. Put aside and keep warm. Melt the margarine in a small saucepan, stir in the breadcrumbs and fry for 2 minutes until golden brown. Remove from the heat and add the parsley, mixing well. Pour over the vegetables, then garnish with the chopped egg.

PEASE PUDDING
Serves 4–6

1 lb (450 g) dried split peas, soaked in cold water for 2 hours
1 oz (25 g) butter
1 egg
1 tbsp chopped fresh mint
salt and freshly ground black pepper

Preheat the oven to 375°F/190°C/Gas Mk 5. Drain the peas and place in a saucepan with sufficient water to cover them. Bring to the boil, then skim off any scum which forms on top of the water. Lower the heat and simmer gently for 1 hour. Drain and leave to cool slightly. Use a blender or food processor to blend the peas to a smooth paste. Mix in the butter, egg, mint and salt and pepper to taste and blend for a further 30 seconds. Put the mixture in a greased 2½ pint (1.4 L) ovenproof dish and bake in the oven for 30–35 minutes.

COURGETTE AND TOMATO CASSEROLE
Serves 4

4 large courgettes, sliced
4 tomatoes, skinned and sliced
1 small onion, finely chopped
a little butter
salt and freshly ground black pepper

Heat the oven to 350°F/180°C/Gas Mk 4. Lightly grease an ovenproof casserole dish and arrange the vegetables in alternate layers in the dish, sprinkling salt and pepper to taste between each layer. Dot with the butter, cover and cook in the oven for 40 minutes until the courgettes are tender.

PEPERONATA
Serves 4

2 tbsp olive oil
1 onion, chopped
4 red peppers, deseeded and sliced
6 tomatoes, peeled and chopped
1 tsp sugar
salt and freshly ground black pepper
1 tbsp chopped fresh parsley

Heat the olive oil in a frying pan and sauté the onion until transparent. Add the peppers, cover and cook over a low heat for 15 minutes. Stir in the tomatoes, sugar, salt and pepper, then cover and cook for a further 15 minutes. Sprinkle with parsley and serve.

CORN FRITTERS
Serves 4–6

2 eggs, separated
6 oz (175 g) sweetcorn
salt
pinch sugar
1 tsp baking powder
4 oz (110 g) fresh breadcrumbs
oil for frying

Beat the egg yolks well, add to the sweetcorn and season with salt and sugar. Whisk the egg whites stiffly and fold in. Add the baking powder and enough breadcrumbs to make the mixture stiff enough to handle. Form into little cakes. Heat some oil in a frying pan and fry the cakes gently until brown on both sides. Serve with Chicken Maryland (see page 50).

AUBERGINES WITH WALNUT SAUCE
Serves 4

4 aubergines, sliced
salt
2 oz (50 g) plain flour
3 fl oz (75 ml) olive oil
1 onion, chopped
2 garlic cloves, chopped or crushed
3 tomatoes, chopped
2 tbsp chopped fresh parsley
6 walnuts, finely chopped

Soak the aubergine slices in salted cold water for 30 minutes. Drain and dry well. Flour the aubergine slices and fry in the hot oil for 3 minutes, turning once. Remove and set aside. Add the onion, garlic, tomatoes and parsley to the pan and cook for 5 minutes, stirring occasionally. Return the aubergines to the pan with the chopped walnuts. Mix together and cook for 10 minutes.

COURGETTES PROVENÇAL
Serves 4

4 tbsp olive oil
1 onion, chopped
1 lb (450 g) courgettes, thinly sliced
1 garlic clove, chopped
4 tomatoes, peeled and chopped
1 tbsp tomato purée
salt and freshly ground black pepper

Heat the oil in large frying pan, and fry the onion and courgettes gently for 8–10 minutes, stirring from time to time. Add the garlic, tomatoes, tomato purée and salt and pepper to taste. Cover and cook over low heat for 5 minutes before serving.

RICE AND LENTIL ROAST
Serves 4

2 oz (50 g) brown rice
4 oz (110 g) red lentils
1 large onion, chopped
1 tbsp oil
4 oz (110 g) ground hazelnuts
1 tsp yeast extract
½ tsp dried sage
1 egg, beaten
salt and freshly ground black pepper

Cook the rice in boiling salted water for 15 minutes. Meanwhile, wash the lentils and cook in boiling salted water for 30–40 minutes, until they are soft but still retain their shape. Preheat the oven to 375°F/190°C/Gas Mk 5. Drain the lentils and the rice. Heat the oil and cook the onion until soft. Mix all the ingredients together and place in a greased baking dish. Bake in the oven for 30–40 minutes.

SALADS AND DRESSINGS

RUSSIAN SALAD
Serves 4–6

8 oz (225 g) potatoes, cooked
8 oz (225 g) carrots, cooked
8 oz (225 g) peas, cooked
8 oz (225 g) green beans, cooked
4 oz (110 g) turnip, cooked

Dressing:
2 tbsp olive oil
1 tbsp white wine vinegar
1 tsp French mustard
salt and freshly ground black pepper
mayonnaise

Dice all the vegetables, except the peas, and put into a large bowl. Mix the oil, white wine vinegar and mustard together and season well. Pour over the mixed vegetables and leave for several hours in a cool place. Turn over gently from time to time. Transfer to a serving dish and spoon over enough mayonnaise to cover.

BEEF COLESLAW
Serves 6

1 lb (450 g) white cabbage
4 tbsp vinegar
1 tbsp sugar
salt and freshly ground black pepper
2 carrots, grated
1 tbsp snipped chives
1 green pepper, deseeded and cut into strips
8 oz (225 g) cooked beef, cut into strips
6 tbsp mayonnaise
¼ pt (150 ml) soured cream

Finely shred the cabbage and place in cold salted water in the fridge for 1 hour. Drain and dry in absorbent kitchen paper. Mix together the vinegar, sugar, salt and pepper in a bowl, add the cabbage and leave for 1 hour. Add the carrots, chives, pepper and beef to the cabbage. Mix together the mayonnaise and sour cream and pour over the salad.

LAMB, APPLE AND RICE SALAD
Serves 6

1 lb (450 g) cooked shoulder of lamb, trimmed of fat and cut into cubes
8 oz (225 g) long-grain rice
1 onion, finely chopped
4 fl oz (125 ml) mayonnaise
1 tbsp lemon juice
salt and freshly ground black pepper
2 dessert apples
½ lettuce
2 oz (50 g) salted peanuts

Prepare the meat. Cook the rice in boiling salted water for 20 minutes. Drain and wash in cold water, drain again and leave to cool. When cold, mix together with the lamb and chopped onion in a bowl. In a separate bowl, mix together the mayonnaise and lemon juice and season with salt and pepper to taste. Stir into the lamb and rice and chill for 1 hour. When ready to serve, finely dice the apples. Place the lettuce leaves on a serving dish, arrange the lamb and rice on top and garnish with the apples and peanuts.

CELERY, BUTTER BEAN AND MUSHROOM SALAD
Serves 4

15 oz (425 g) can butter beans, drained and rinsed
2 oz (50 g) button mushrooms, thinly sliced
2 large spring onions, finely chopped
4 celery stalks, thinly sliced
1½ tsp wine vinegar
1½ tsp peppercorn mustard
3 tbsp oil
2 tbsp double cream
1 tbsp chopped fresh parsley
salt and freshly ground black pepper

Mix together the butter beans, mushrooms, spring onion and celery in a large salad bowl and set aside. Whisk together the vinegar and mustard, then whisk in the oil. When the mixture is thoroughly blended, whisk in the cream and parsley and salt and pepper to taste. Pour over the vegetables, turning gently until they are coated with the dressing. Leave to stand for 20 minutes before serving.

TURKEY AND AVOCADO SALAD
Serves 4

2 avocados
fresh orange juice
½ small red pepper, deseeded
½ small green pepper, deseeded
8 oz (225 g) cooked turkey, diced
1–2 tsp Worcester sauce
2–3 tbsp mayonnaise
salt and freshly ground black pepper

Peel and stone the avocados, slice and arrange in a circle on a serving dish. Brush over the orange juice. Cut a few thin slices from the green and the red peppers to use for garnish and chop the remainder. In a bowl, mix the turkey with the chopped peppers, Worcestershire sauce and the mayonnaise. Add salt and pepper to taste. Pile this mixture into the centre of the serving dish and place the pepper slices on top. Chill well before serving.

TURKEY PASTA SALAD
Serves 6

6 oz (175 g) small pasta shapes
1 tbsp olive oil
1½ lb (675 g) cold cooked turkey, diced
2 oz (50 g) sultanas
2 tbsp chopped fresh chives
4 oz (110 g) button mushrooms
2 oz (50 g) walnuts, chopped
1 small red pepper, deseeded and chopped
1 small yellow pepper, deseeded and chopped
salt and freshly ground black pepper
¼ pt (150 ml) French dressing (see page 140)

Cook the pasta until *al dente* then drain and cool under cold running water. Drain thoroughly, and tip into a large bowl with the oil and mix well. Add the turkey, sultanas and chives to the pasta and mix. Place the mushrooms in a bowl of boiling water and leave for 5 minutes, then drain thoroughly and slice finely. Add to the mixture together with the walnuts and peppers and season well. Pour over the French dressing and toss until all the ingredients are well mixed. Cover the bowl with cling film and refrigerate for several hours before serving.

AUTUMN CHUTNEY
Makes about 4–5 lb (2.5 kg)

3 lb (1.4 kg) cooking or windfall apples
1 lb (450 g) pears
2 lb (900 g) red tomatoes, skinned, deseeded and chopped
1 lb (450 g) chopped dates
1 pt (600 ml) malt vinegar
2 lb (900 g) soft brown sugar
1 tsp cayenne pepper
2 tsp mixed spice
1 tbsp salt
1 tsp freshly ground black pepper

Peel, core and roughly chop the apples and pears. Put the tomato flesh with all the other ingredients in a preserving pan and simmer over a moderate heat for about 2 hours or until the fruit is tender and the chutney is thick enough to separate when a wooden spoon is drawn through it. Spoon the chutney into hot sterilised jars, seal, cover tightly, label and date.

TURKEY AND RICE SALAD
Serves 6

8 oz (225 g) brown rice
1½ lb (675 g) cold cooked turkey, diced
8 oz (225 g) fresh pineapple, chopped
2 oz (50 g) sultanas
2 tbsp chopped fresh chives
4 oz (110 g) button mushrooms
2 oz (50 g) cashew nuts
1 small red pepper, deseeded and chopped
1 small yellow pepper, deseeded and chopped
¼ pt (150 ml) French dressing (see page 140)

Cook the rice as directed on the packet. Drain thoroughly, rinse in cold water and drain again. Place the turkey, pineapple, sultanas and chives in a large bowl and mix in the rice. Place the mushrooms in a bowl of boiling water and leave for 5 minutes, then drain thoroughly and slice finely. Add to the rice mixture together with the cashew nuts and peppers. Pour over the French dressing and toss until all the ingredients are well blended. Cover the bowl with clingfilm and refrigerate for several hours before serving.

SCANDINAVIAN CHICKEN SALAD
Serves 4

12–16 oz (350–450 g) chicken, cooked
4 eggs, hard-boiled
2 tbsp horseradish sauce
½ tbsp lemon juice
6 tbsp whipped cream
salt and freshly ground black pepper
lettuce leaves

Chop the chicken into cubes. Chop or mash the eggs with a fork. Put in a bowl, add the horseradish sauce and lemon juice and mix well. Mix in the cream. Add the chicken cubes and salt and pepper to taste. Stir well. Place the lettuce leaves on a serving dish and pile the chicken mixture on top.

MAYONNAISE
Makes about 6 fl oz (175 ml)

1 egg yolk
good pinch salt and pepper
¼ tsp dry or made mustard
¼ pt (150 ml) salad oil
1 tbsp vinegar

Put the egg yolk and seasonings into a basin. Gradually beat in the oil drop by drop, stirring all the time, preferably with an electric whisk, until the mixture is thick. When it becomes creamy, stop adding oil, as too much oil will make it curdle. Beat in the vinegar gradually, then 1 tbsp warm water. Use the same day.

RED TOMATO DRESSING
Makes about ½ pt (300 ml)

½ pt (300 ml) tomato juice
1 tbsp tarragon vinegar
1 garlic clove, crushed
salt and freshly ground black pepper

Place the tomato juice, tarragon, vinegar and garlic in a jar with a secure screw top and shake well. Add salt and pepper to taste.

135

HERB VINAIGRETTE
Makes ¼ pt (125 ml) dressing

salt and freshly ground black pepper
½ tsp Dijon mustard
½ tsp sugar
2 tbsp white wine vinegar
6 tbsp olive oil
½ tbsp lemon juice
1 tsp chopped fresh tarragon
1 tsp chopped fresh chervil
1 tsp chopped fresh dill
2 tsp chopped fresh chives
1 garlic clove

Mix together the mustard, sugar, and vinegar and season to taste with salt and pepper. Stir well. Gradually beat in the oil using a wooden spoon. Add the lemon juice and stir in the herbs. Add the whole garlic clove and leave for 1 hour. Remove the garlic and use as required. Chill before using.

WINTER VEGETABLE SALAD
Serves 6

2 medium carrots, diced
1 small turnip, diced
4 oz (110 g) French beans, chopped
4 tbsp French dressing (see page 140)
2 medium potatoes
¼ pt (150 ml) mayonnaise
1 egg, hard-boiled
1 tbsp chopped fresh parsley

Place the carrots, turnip and beans in salted water and boil until almost tender. Drain well and toss in French dressing while still warm. Leave the skins on the potatoes and cook in boiling water until tender. Drain, leave to cool, then remove the skins and cut into cubes. When completely cold, place in a bowl and add the carrots, turnip and beans, Pour in the mayonnaise and toss well. Cut the egg into quarters and arrange on top of the salad. Sprinkle over the parsley.

JELLIED BEETROOT AND APPLE SALAD
Serves 6

1 packet red jelly
½ pt (300 ml) boiling water
¼ pt (150 ml) vinegar
2 tbsp lemon juice
1 lb (450 g) cooked beetroot
2 crisp eating apples
2 oz (50 g) shelled walnuts
lettuce or watercress, optional

Break up the jelly tablet and dissolve in the boiling water. Mix together the vinegar and lemon juice, make this up to ½ pt (300 ml) with cold water and add this liquid to the hot jelly liquid. Peel and slice the cooked beetroot. Peel, core and slice the apples. Place the walnuts in the base of a 2 pint (1.2 L) ring mould and add the beetroot and apple in layers. Pour over the liquid jelly and leave in a cool place to set. To serve, unmould onto a flat dish and surround with lettuce or watercress.

AVOCADO AND PRAWN SALAD
Serves 4

2 ripe avocado pears
lemon juice
1 iceberg lettuce
1 lb (450 g) peeled prawns
½ cucumber, sliced
8 radishes, sliced
1 lemon, sliced

Peel the avocados, cut in half and remove the stones. Slice, place in a bowl and sprinkle with lemon juice to prevent discoloration. Remove the outer leaves from the lettuce and arrange on a serving dish. Chop the lettuce heart into wedges and place in a bowl together with the prawns, cucumber, radishes and lemon. Gently mix together and then pile on top of the lettuce leaves. Arrange the avocado slices around the edge of the prawn mixture.

SPANISH ONION SALAD
Serves 4

2 large Spanish onions, thinly sliced
1 red pepper, deseeded and thinly sliced
1 green chilli, finely chopped
2 tbsp oil
1 tbsp lemon juice
½ tsp Dijon mustard
salt and freshly ground black pepper
½ tsp ground coriander
1 tbsp chopped fresh parsley

Place the onion, pepper and chilli in a serving dish. Mix together the oil, lemon juice, mustard, coriander and salt and pepper to taste and pour over the salad. Cover and chill in the refrigerator for 1 hour. Sprinkle with parsley and serve.

CORNED BEEF AND CUCUMBER SALAD
Serves 4

8 oz (225 g) corned beef, diced
8 oz (225 g) new potatoes, cooked and diced
2 oz (50 g) gherkin, chopped
4 tbsp mayonnaise
4 large lettuce leaves

Mix together the beef, potato and gherkin in a large bowl. Stir in the mayonnaise until all the ingredients are well coated. Arrange the lettuce leaves on four serving plates and divide the meat and potato mixture between the four plates.

GREEN SALAD WITH FETA CHEESE
Serves 4

2 oz (50 g) black olives
1 small cos lettuce
½ cucumber, thickly sliced
1 small green pepper, deseeded and sliced
1 small bunch watercress
4 tbsp French dressing (see page 140)
4 oz (110 g) feta cheese, cubed
1 tbsp chopped fresh parsley

Place the olives in a bowl. Break up the lettuce into small pieces and add to the bowl together with the cucumber, pepper and watercress. Pour on the French dressing, toss well and arrange the feta cheese on top. Garnish with parsley and serve.

TURKEY AND CELERY SALAD
Serves 4

3 lb (1.4 kg) cooked turkey, diced
1 celery stalk, finely chopped
Dressing:
4 tbsp olive oil
2 tbsp white wine vinegar
pinch mustard
½ tsp sugar
salt and freshly ground black pepper
2 tsp chopped fresh chives
2 oz (50 g) smoked ham, chopped

Place the turkey and celery in a bowl and chill for one hour. In another bowl, mix the oil, vinegar, mustard, sugar, salt and pepper and mix well. Pour over the turkey and celery, add the chives and mix well. Pile into a serving dish and garnish with the chopped ham.

WELSH SALAD
Serves 6

4 medium leeks, trimmed
1 lettuce
6 medium tomatoes
small bunch radishes
¼ pt (150 ml) whipping cream
¼ pt (150 ml) mayonnaise
salt and freshly ground black pepper

Slice the leeks into ½ inch (1 cm) pieces, separate into rings and wash well. Drain. Shred the lettuce, chop the tomatoes into wedges and trim and slice the radishes. Place all of them in a serving bowl. Whip the cream and add the mayonnaise and salt and pepper to taste. Pour over the salad and toss lightly.

FRENCH DRESSING
Makes ½ pt (300 ml)

6 fl oz (175 ml) olive or salad oil
4 fl oz (125 ml) wine vinegar
¼ tsp French mustard
salt and freshly ground black pepper
pinch sugar

Place all the ingredients in a clean screw top jar and shake vigorously before use. Use for all types of salad. The proportions are 3–4 times oil to vinegar depending on taste and the dressing can be flavoured with crushed garlic or finely chopped fresh herbs.

ROSY APPLE CHUTNEY
Makes 2½ lb (1.1 kg)

1½ lb (675 g) cooking apples or windfalls, peeled, cored and sliced
8 oz (225 g) onions, chopped
½ pt (300 ml) malt vinegar
8 oz (225 g) granulated sugar
1 lb (450 g) cooked beetroot, peeled, sliced and diced

Put the apples and onions in a preserving pan. Cover with half the vinegar and simmer over a gentle heat until soft. Add the remaining vinegar, the sugar and the beetroot and cook until thick, stirring from time to time. Leave to cool slightly, then spoon into hot, sterilised jars, cover, seal and label.

CHICKEN AND AVOCADO SALAD
Serves 4

2 ripe avocado
lemon juice
2 tbsp apple juice
2 tbsp horseradish sauce
2 tbsp mayonnaise
salt and freshly ground black pepper
6 baby beetroots, sliced
8 slices cold cooked chicken breast

Peel the avocados, cut in half, remove the stones and chop. Put them in a bowl and pour over the lemon juice to prevent discoloration. Put the apple juice, horseradish sauce and mayonnaise in a bowl, add salt and pepper to taste and mix well. Mix in the avocados. Arrange the beetroot and chicken alternately around the edge of a flat serving dish and pile the avocado mixture in the centre.

LETTUCE AND GRAPE SALAD
Serves 6

1 small iceberg lettuce
3 celery stalks, sliced
1 dessert apple, sliced
juice of ½ lemon
4 oz (110 g) seedless green grapes
1 oz (25 g) walnuts, chopped
4 tbsp French dressing (see page 140)
black grapes, to garnish

Shred the lettuce and arrange in a salad bowl. Add the celery. Dip the apple slices in lemon juice to prevent discoloration and then add to the bowl together with the green grapes and the walnuts. Pour over the French dressing, toss well and garnish with black grapes to serve.

SPICY HERRING SALAD
Serves 4

4 oz (110 g) pickled herrings, cut into strips
1 small onion, grated
2 hard-boiled eggs, chopped
¼ pt (150 ml) soured cream
2 tsp lemon juice
salt and freshly ground black pepper
paprika
8 oz (225 g) cooked new potatoes, diced

Place all the ingredients in a large salad bowl and mix well together. Set aside in a cool place for about 1 hour before serving.

GREEK SALAD
Serves 4

2 oz (50 g) black or green olives
1 small lettuce
½ cucumber, thickly sliced
1 small green pepper, deseeded and sliced
4 tbsp French dressing (see page 140)
1 lb (450 g) ripe tomatoes, cut into wedges
4 oz (110 g) feta cheese, cubed
4 spring onions, finely chopped
1 tbsp chopped fresh parsley

Put the olives in a large bowl. Break the lettuce into small pieces and add to the bowl together with the cucumber and pepper. Pour over the French dressing and toss well. Arrange the tomato wedges and feta cheese around and on top of the salad. Sprinkle with spring onion and parsley.

APPLESLAW
Serves 4

1 eating apple, coarsely grated
1 tsp lemon juice
1 large carrot, coarsely grated
8 oz (225 g) white cabbage, finely shredded
1–2 tbsp apple juice
2 tbsp quark or curd cheese
freshly ground black pepper

Put the apple in a bowl and sprinkle over the lemon juice. Mix gently until the apple is well coated with the juice. Mix in the carrot and cabbage. Mix the apple juice and quark to a smooth creamy consistency and pour over the salad. Sprinkle with pepper to taste.

CRAB SALAD
Serves 2

8 oz (225 g) cooked crab meat
½ cucumber
2 tomatoes, chopped
2 oz (50 g) pasta shells, cooked
1 tbsp lemon juice
1 tbsp mayonnaise
1 tbsp yoghurt
freshly ground black pepper
1 lettuce, shredded

Put the crab, cucumber, tomatoes and pasta shells in a bowl and mix well. In another bowl, mix together the lemon juice, mayonnaise and yoghurt. Pour over the crab mixture and combine well, adding pepper to taste. Arrange the shredded lettuce in a serving dish and pile the crab mixture on top.

SAUSAGE AND PASTA SALAD
Serves 4

8 oz (225 g) pasta shapes, cooked
8 oz (225 g) beer sausage (Bierwurst), cut into strips
4 oz (110 g) mushrooms, sliced
4 oz (110 g) celery, finely chopped
1 red pepper, deseeded and cut into strips
4 tsp mayonnaise
2 tsp creamed horseradish
1 tsp German mustard
lettuce leaves

Place the pasta, sausage, mushrooms, celery and red pepper in a large salad bowl and mix well. In a small bowl, mix together the mayonnaise, horseradish and mustard. Pour over the salad ingredients and toss well. Serve on a bed of lettuce leaves.

PUDDINGS

LOGANBERRY AND APPLE CRUMBLE
Serves 6

2 oz (50 g) plain flour, sifted
2 oz (50 g) wholemeal flour
2 oz (50 g) ground almonds
3 oz (75 g) margarine
2 oz (50 g) light Muscovado sugar
1 lb (450 g) apples, stewed and sweetened to taste with honey
12 oz (350 g) loganberries
1 oz (25 g) flaked almonds

Preheat the oven to 400°F/200°C/Gas Mk 6. Place both the flours in a bowl together with the ground almonds and rub in the margarine until the mixture resembles fine breadcrumbs. Mix in the sugar. Place the apples and loganberries in a bowl and mix well. Arrange evenly in a pie dish, spoon over the crumble mixture and sprinkle the top with flaked almonds. Bake in the oven for 30 minutes until golden brown.

RHUBARB SPONGE
Serves 4

4 oz (110 g) cooked rhubarb
2 oz (50 g) butter
2 oz (50 g) caster sugar
1 egg
4 oz (110 g) plain flour, sifted
pinch salt
½ tsp baking powder

Preheat the oven to 400°F/200°C/Gas Mk 6. Butter a pie dish and layer the cooked rhubarb in it. Add sugar to sweeten if desired. Beat the butter and sugar until thick and creamy, then beat in the egg. Sift in the flour, salt and baking powder gradually and blend in lightly. If the mixture appears to be too thick, add a little milk. Spread the sponge mixture over the rhubarb, and cook in the centre of the oven for about 20 minutes or until set and golden. Serve hot or cold with custard or cream. This pudding can also be made with cooked apple or pears instead of rhubarb.

SUMMER PUDDING
Serves 6

8 large slices bread, crusts removed
8 oz (225 g) rhubarb
8 oz (225 g) mixed redcurrants and blackcurrants
4 oz (110 g) honey
6 tbsp water
8 oz (225 g) small strawberries
8 oz (225 g) loganberries or raspberries

Reserve one slice of bread and use the rest to line the base and sides of a 2 pint (1.2 L) fairly shallow round dish. Chop the rhubarb into slices and put in a saucepan together with the currants. Pour in the honey and water, bring to the boil and simmer for a few minutes, stirring from time to time, until the fruit is soft. Add the strawberries and loganberries and cook for 1 minute. Pour the mixture into the bread lined dish and place the remaining slice of bread on top. Bend over the bread from the sides to seal with the slice on top. Place a plate on top of the pudding, pressing down until the fruit juice rises to the top of the dish. Place something fairly heavy on top to weigh down the pudding and leave in the refrigerator overnight. Turn out upside-down onto a flat dish to serve.

FRUIT AND NUT CRUMBLE
Serves 4

4 oz (110 g) plain flour, sifted
pinch salt
2 oz (50 g) butter
4 oz (110 g) demerara sugar
1 oz (25 g) walnuts, finely chopped
2 tbsp redcurrant jelly
finely grated rind and juice of 1 lemon
3 cooking pears, peeled, cored and sliced
1 large cooking apple, peeled, cored and sliced

Preheat the oven to 350°F/180°C/Gas Mk 4. Mix together the flour and salt in a bowl. Rub in the butter. Add the walnuts and half of the sugar. Place the redcurrant jelly, lemon juice and rind and remaining sugar in a bowl and mix well. Fold in the fruit. Place this mixture in an ovenproof dish and top with the crumble mixture. Bake for 40 minutes until the topping is crisp and golden. Serve hot.

BANANA PUDDING
Serves 6

6 ripe bananas
2 oz (50 g) margarine or butter
4 oz (110 g) light Muscavado sugar
3 oz (75 g) self-raising flour, sifted
1 oz (25 g) wholemeal flour
1 egg, beaten
good pinch mixed spice

Preheat the oven to 350°F/180°C/Gas Mk 4. Peel and mash the bananas in a bowl. Melt the margarine then pour over the bananas. Add the sugar, flours, egg and spice and mix thoroughly until well blended. Place the mixture in a lightly greased 2 pint (1.2 L) ovenproof dish and bake in the oven for 45 minutes until the pudding has shrunk from the sides of the dish and is golden brown. Serve hot.

JAM SUET PUDDING
Serves 4

4 oz (110 g) self-raising flour, sifted
pinch salt
2 oz (50 g) sugar
2 oz (50 g) shredded suet
2 tbsp milk
4 tbsp jam of choice

Mix the flour and salt together in a bowl. Add the sugar and shredded suet and blend well. Gradually stir in the milk, blending until the mixture is firm. Grease a 1 pint (600 ml) pudding basin. Line the base with two-thirds of the pastry and put the jam in the bottom. Cover the pudding with the remaining pastry, then cover with greased greaseproof paper making a pleat across the top for the pudding to rise. Secure the paper around the basin with string. Place the basin over a saucepan of water and boil for 1½ hours. Turn out onto a warm serving dish and heat some extra jam or make custard to pour over the top.

RAISIN RICE
Serves 4

1 pt (600 ml) milk
2 oz (50 g) short-grain rice, washed
2 oz (50 g) caster sugar
2 egg yolks, beaten
¼ tsp vanilla essence
2 oz (50 g) seedless raisins

Topping:
2 egg whites
½ oz (10 g) caster sugar

Preheat the oven to 400°F/200°C/Gas Mk 6. Put the milk in a saucepan and bring to the boil. Sprinkle in the rice. Stir until the milk comes back to the boil, then stir in the sugar. Lower the heat and simmer very gently, covered, for 30–35 minutes or until thick and creamy. Take the pan off the heat and stir in the egg yolks, vanilla essence and raisins. Butter a 2 pint (1.2 L) pie dish and pour in the rice. To make the topping, beat the egg whites until stiff and shiny and then gradually whisk in the sugar. Spoon over the hot pudding and put in the middle of the oven. Bake for about 5 minutes until golden brown. Serve at once with cream.

LEMON RICE PUDDING
Serves 6

3 oz (75 g) short-grain rice
3 oz (75 g) caster sugar
grated rind of 1 lemon
2 pt (1.2 L) full-cream milk
2 oz (50 g) butter

Preheat the oven to 330°F/180°C/Gas Mk 4. Place the rice, sugar and lemon rind in a well-buttered ovenproof dish and pour over the milk. Bake for 1 hour, stirring occasionally. Decrease the temperature to 325°F/170°C/Gas Mk 3 and bake for ¾–1 hour. Dot with butter to serve.

SWISS TRIFLE BAKE
Serves 4

1 Swiss roll
14 oz (400 g) can apricots, drained
2 tbsp custard powder
2 eggs, separated
1 tbsp granulated sugar
1 pt (600 ml) milk
4 oz (110 g) caster sugar
1 oz (25 g) almonds, blanched and halved

Preheat the oven to 350°F/180°C/Gas Mk 4. Slice the Swiss roll and place in a 2 pt (1.2 L) ovenproof dish. Arrange the apricots on top. Blend the custard powder, egg yolks and granulated sugar in a bowl, with a little of the milk. Heat the remaining milk in a small saucepan and when nearly at boiling point, pour onto the custard mixture, stirring. Pour back into the saucepan and bring to the boil, stirring constantly until thickened, then pour over the apricots and Swiss roll. Whisk the egg whites in a bowl until stiff and gradually whisk in the caster sugar. Pile this mixture on top of the custard and sprinkle with almonds. Bake in the oven for 20 minutes until the top is golden brown.

CREAMED RICE
Serves 4

3 oz (75 g) short-grain rice
1 pt (600 ml) milk
1 oz (25 g) sugar
1 egg, separated
½ oz (10 g) butter
1 packet orange jelly
glacé cherries, halved

Place the rice, milk and sugar in a large saucepan. Stir and bring to the boil, reduce heat, cover and simmer for 30 minutes, stirring occasionally. Lightly beat the egg yolk and stir into the mixture together with the butter. Remove from the heat. Dissolve the jelly in ¼ pt (150 ml) boiling water. When cool, stir into the rice. Whisk the egg white until stiff then fold into the rice mixture. Lightly oil a ring mould and press in the mixture. Chill until well set. To serve, turn out onto a dish and decorate with glacé cherries.

CARAMEL RICE
Serves 4

1 pt (600 ml) milk
3 oz (75 g) short-grain rice
2 oz (50 g) granulated sugar
2 oz (50 g) caster sugar
2 eggs, beaten
few drops of vanilla essence

Preheat the oven to 400°F/200°C/Gas Mk 6. In a large saucepan, heat the milk and bring to the boil. Stir in the rice. Cover and simmer over low heat for 30 minutes until the rice is soft, stirring occasionally. In the meantime, place the granulated sugar in a small saucepan with 2–3 tablespoons water and cook over low heat. Bring to the boil and cook quickly until caramel coloured. Remove from the heat, wait until the bubbles subside, then pour into a shallow, ovenproof dish, coating the base and sides with the caramel. Remove the rice from the heat and stir in the caster sugar, eggs and vanilla essence. Pour into the dish and bake in the oven for 20–30 minutes until set.

APRICOT RICE CREAM
Serves 6

3 oz (75 g) short-grain rice
1½ pt (900 ml) milk
2–3 drops vanilla essence
1 egg white
¼ pt (150 ml) double cream, whipped into soft peaks
3 oz (75 g) caster sugar
14 oz (400 g) can apricots in natural juice
2 tbsp Kirsch
2 oz (50 g) flaked almonds, lightly toasted

Preheat the oven to 325°F/160°C/Gas Mk 3. Place the rice, milk and vanilla essence in a saucepan and bring to the boil, stirring constantly. Lower the heat and simmer for 40–45 minutes until the rice is soft and most of the liquid has been absorbed. Remove from the heat and leave to cool slightly. Whisk the egg white to form soft peaks and fold into the rice. Fold in the whipped cream together with 2 oz (50 g) of the sugar. Pile the rice mixture into an ovenproof dish. Make a purée of the apricots in a blender, then stir in the remaining sugar and the Kirsch. Spoon the purée over the top of the rice and sprinkle over the almonds. Cook in the oven for 15 minutes and serve.

GOLDEN SYRUP PUDDING
Serves 4

4 oz (110 g) margarine
4 oz (110 g) caster sugar
2 large eggs
4 oz (110 g) self-raising flour, sifted
2–3 tbsp golden syrup

Cream the margarine and sugar in a bowl, until soft and fluffy. Gradually beat in the eggs and, if necessary, add a little of the flour if the mixture starts to curdle. Fold in the remaining flour and mix well. Grease a 1½ pint (900 ml) pudding basin and pour the syrup over the base. Pile the pudding mixture on top and cover with greased greaseproof paper making a pleat cross the top. Secure the paper around the basin with string. Place over a saucepan of boiling water and steam for 1½ hours. Turn out onto a warm dish and heat extra syrup to pour over the top to serve.

RHUBARB AND DATE BAKE
Serves 4

4 oz (110 g) plain flour, sifted
pinch salt
2 tsp cocoa powder
2 oz (50 g) margarine or butter
1 tbsp golden syrup
2 oz (50 g) dates
3 sticks rhubarb, cut into 1 in (2.5 cm) pieces
milk to mix

Preheat the oven to 425°F/220°C/Gas Mk 7. Sift the flour, salt and cocoa into a bowl and rub in the butter or margarine. Warm the syrup and add it to the mixture, then add the chopped dates and rhubarb. Mix with the milk to a thick batter. Pour into a greased baking tin and bake in a preheated oven for 20–30 minutes. Serve hot with cream or custard.

SOUTHERN PEARS
Serves 4

1½ lb (675 g) cooking pears
4 oz (110 g) honey
½ pt (300 ml) sweet cider
4 cloves

Peel, quarter and core the pears. Pour the honey and cider into a saucepan and add the cloves. Carefully arrange the pears in the saucepan, cover and simmer gently over low heat for 30 minutes until the pears are tender. Remove the cloves and serve the pears on a warmed dish.

BAKED APPLE DUMPLINGS
Serves 4

8 oz (225 g) shortcrust pastry
4 small cooking apples
1 oz (25 g) seedless raisins
½ oz (15 g) brown sugar
½ oz (15 g) butter
¼ tsp cinnamon
beaten egg or milk, for glazing
caster sugar, for dusting

Preheat the oven to 425°F/220°C/Gas Mk 7. Make the pastry in the usual way and roll out on a lightly floured board. Cut out four circles using a saucer as a template. Peel and core the apples and place one in the centre of each pastry round. Mix the raisins, sugar, butter and cinnamon, and fill the centre of each apple with the mixture. Fold the pastry up around each apple and squeeze the top together using a little water to seal. Invert on a baking tray and brush with a little beaten egg or milk. Bake for 25 minutes or until really golden brown. Dust with caster sugar and serve hot with cream.

BREAD AND BUTTER PUDDING
Serves 4

3 slices bread, buttered
2–3 oz (50–75 g) sultanas
2 eggs
1½ oz (35 g) sugar
¾ pt (450 ml) milk

Preheat the oven to 350°F/180°C/Gas Mk 4. Cut the buttered bread into triangles. Lightly grease a 2 pint (1.2 L) pie dish. Arrange the triangles of bread in the dish, sprinkling sultanas between the bread slices, and some sultanas over the top. Beat together the eggs and sugar. Warm the milk, pour over the egg mixture and beat until well blended. Pour over the bread and sultanas. Leave to stand for a short time before baking in the oven for 45 minutes until set. Serve hot.

ORANGE SPONGE TART
Serves 4

6 oz (175 g) shortcrust pastry
3 tbsp thin-cut orange marmalade
3 oz (75 g) butter, cut into small pieces
3 oz (75 g) caster sugar
1 egg
2 tsp finely grated orange rind
1 oz (25 g) ground almonds
4 oz (110 g) self-raising flour, sifted
2 tbsp orange juice
1½ oz (35 g) almond halves or slivers

Preheat the oven to 425°F/220°C/Gas Mk 7. Roll out the pastry on a
lightly floured board and use to line a 7 inch (17.5 cm) ovenproof pie
plate. Spread the base with the orange marmalade. Cream the butter
and sugar together until light and fluffy, beat in the egg, stir in the
orange rind and almonds, and then fold in the flour alternately with
the orange juice. Put the mixture into the pastry case, spread evenly
with a knife and decorate with the almonds. Bake in the oven for
20 minutes and then reduce the heat to 325°F/170°C/Gas Mk 3 for
20 minutes. Serve hot or cold.

RHUBARB AND ORANGE FUDGE CRUMBLE
Serves 6

1½ lb (675 g) rhubarb
5 oz (150 g) soft brown sugar
juice of 2 oranges
4 oz (110 g) butter
4 oz (110 g) demerara sugar
10 digestive biscuits, crushed
1 tsp vanilla essence
grated rind of 1 orange

Preheat the oven to 350°F/180°C/Gas Mk 4. Put the rhubarb, sugar
and orange juice in a saucepan and cook over medium heat for
15 minutes until the rhubarb is tender. Put into an ovenproof dish.
Heat the butter and sugar together in a saucepan until the butter has
melted. Stir in the biscuits, add the vanilla essence and orange rind and
blend thoroughly. Spread the mixture over the rhubarb and bake in
the oven for 20–25 minutes.

GOOSEBERRY ROLL
Serves 4

8 oz (225 g) plain flour, sifted
1 tsp baking powder
2 oz (50 g) shredded suet or grated margarine
golden syrup
6 oz (175 g) gooseberries, topped and tailed

Preheat the oven to 375°F/190°C/Gas Mk 5. Mix together the flour and baking powder and stir in the suet or margarine. Mix with sufficient cold water to form a stiff dough. Roll out on a lightly floured board into an oblong shape and spread with the golden syrup. Place a layer of gooseberries over the syrup leaving a border of about ½ inch (1 cm) around the edge. Brush this border with water and roll up the pastry sealing the ends firmly. Place in a large baking tin or dish and bake in the oven for 1 hour until cooked through and golden. Serve hot with custard or cream.

RHUBARB AND ORANGE CHIFFON PIE
Serves 6

6 oz (175 g) digestive biscuits, crushed
2 oz (50 g) demerara sugar
3 oz (75 g) unsalted butter, melted
1 lb (450 g) rhubarb, cut into 1 in (2.5 cm) lengths
grated rind and juice of 1 large orange
2 eggs, separated
2 oz (50 g) caster sugar
2 tbsp cornflour
½ tsp ground ginger
orange slices, to decorate

Put the biscuits and demerara sugar in a bowl and mix well. Mix in the butter. Press the mixture evenly on the base and up the sides of an 8 inch (20 cm) fluted flan dish. Chill in the refrigerator. Meanwhile, put the rhubarb in a saucepan with 3 tbsp water, cover and cook over low heat, stirring from time to time until the fruit is soft. Purée in a blender or by passing through a sieve and pour into a bowl. Put the orange rind and juice in a heavy-based saucepan and stir in the egg yolks, caster sugar, cornflour and ginger. Cook over low heat, stirring constantly, until thick. Remove from the heat and add to the rhubarb purée, stirring well. Whisk the egg whites until they form stiff peaks and fold into the rhubarb mixture. Arrange on the biscuit crust and chill in the refrigerator overnight. Decorate with the orange slices.

UPSIDE-DOWN APPLE TART
Serves 4

5 oz (150 g) butter
5 oz (150 g) self-raising flour, sifted
4 oz (110 g) + 2 tsp caster sugar
2 lb (900 g) eating apples

Preheat the oven to 400°F/200°C/Gas Mk 6. Rub 3 oz (75 g) of the butter into the flour with the 2 tsp of sugar and mix to a dough with a little cold water. Grease a 7 inch (17.5 cm) round cake tin or ovenproof dish and sprinkle with 2 oz (50 g) caster sugar. Peel and core the apples, cut into slices and place a layer in the base of the dish. Sprinkle with the remaining sugar and then place another layer of apples on top. Roll out the pastry on a lightly floured board to about ⅛ inch (35 mm) thick and place on top of the apples, pushing the pastry neatly round the edges and allowing the excess pastry to fall back inside. Bake in the oven for 10 minutes, then turn the heat down to 375°F/190°C/Gas Mk 5 and bake for a further 30 minutes. Turn out onto a hot serving dish and serve with cream.

PINEAPPLE RICE
Serves 4

1 pt (600 ml) milk
2 oz (50 g) short-grain rice, washed
2 oz (50 g) caster sugar
1 egg, separated
8 oz (225 g) can pineapple pieces
juice of ½ lemon
¼ pt (150 ml) double cream
2 oz (50 g) plain chocolate

Rinse a saucepan, pour in the milk and bring to the boil. Then sprinkle over the rice. Bring back to the boil, stirring, then lower the heat and simmer gently, covered, for about 30 minutes or until the mixture is thick and creamy. Take the pan off the heat and stir in the sugar, beaten egg yolk, pineapple pieces and lemon juice. Put aside to cool with a round of dampened greaseproof paper on top to prevent a skin forming. Whip the cream until thick. Whip the egg white until it forms stiff peaks and fold the cream and egg white gently into the rice and pineapple mixture. Spoon into a serving dish and sprinkle with grated chocolate. Chill for a few hours until ready to serve.

APPLE AND DAMSON TANSY
Serves 4

2 large Cox's apples, peeled, cored and thinly sliced
8 oz (225 g) damsons, halved, stoned and quartered
½ oz (10 g) butter
1½ oz (35 g) sugar
¼ tsp each of ground cloves and cinnamon
4 eggs, separated
3 tbsp soured cream

Put the apples, damsons, butter and half the sugar in a large frying pan. Cook over low heat until all the fruit is soft, stirring constantly. Stir in the spices and remove from the heat. Beat the egg yolks and cream together in a bowl, then stir into the fruit mixture. Whisk the egg whites until they form stiff peaks and fold into the mixture. Return to low heat and cook until the mixture has set. Sprinkle the remaining sugar on top, then brown under a hot grill. Serve immediately from the frying pan.

APPLE AND WALNUT SURPRISE
Serves 6

4 oz (110 g) self-raising flour, sifted
2 oz (50 g) butter, melted
1 egg, beaten
1 tsp vanilla essence
2 tsp grated lemon rind
3 oz (75 g) caster sugar
6 oz (175 g) stoned dates, chopped
2 tbsp chopped walnuts
4 medium cooking apples, peeled, cored and chopped

Preheat the oven to 400°F/200°C/Gas Mk 6. Put the flour in a bowl. Make a well in the centre and pour in the butter, egg, vanilla essence and lemon rind. Mix thoroughly using a wooden spoon. Add the sugar, dates, walnuts and apples and mix well. Put the mixture in a greased shallow ovenproof dish and bake in the oven for 50–60 minutes until risen and deep golden brown in colour. Cut into squares and serve.

MOUNTAIN PUDDING
Serves 4

4 oz (110 g) ratafia biscuits, crushed coarsely
grated rind of 1 lemon
2 oz (50 g) butter
1½ oz (35 g) plain flour
1 pt (600 ml) milk
pinch salt
3 oz (75 g) caster sugar
2 eggs, separated

Heat the oven to 275°F/140°C/Gas Mk 1. Grease a pie dish with
butter and put the ratafias in the base. Sprinkle over the lemon rind.
Make a sweet white sauce using the remaining butter, the flour, milk,
salt and 1 oz (25 g) of the caster sugar. Beat the egg yolks well and stir
into the white sauce. Pour over the ratafias. Whip the egg whites until
they form stiff peaks and whisk in half the remaining caster sugar.
Whip again folding in the remainder of the sugar. Pile on top of the
pudding and bake in the oven for 1¼ hours.

APPLES WITH CINNAMON
Serves 4

3 lb (1.4 kg) apples
7 oz (200 g) sugar
4 fl oz (125 ml) sweet sherry
grated rind and juice of 1 lemon
1 vanilla pod
1 cinnamon stick
icing sugar for dusting

Wash the apples but do not peel them. Remove the stalks and the
cores. Place in a saucepan with enough water to just cover them and
add the sugar, sherry, lemon rind and juice, vanilla pod and cinnamon
stick. Cook over a low heat until the apples begin to go soft. Remove
the apples from the pan and place on a serving dish. Boil the cooking
liquid over a high heat until it has reduced and become syrupy, then
strain the liquid over the apples. Dust with sifted icing sugar.

GOOSEBERRY AND ELDERFLOWER CRUMBLE
Serves 4–6

1 lb (450 g) gooseberries, topped and tailed
3 large heads fresh elderflowers or 2 tsp dried
3 oz (75 g) caster sugar
2 oz (50 g) rolled oats
4 oz (110 g) fresh wholemeal breadcrumbs
2 oz (50 g) butter

Preheat the oven to 350°F/180°C/Gas Mk 4. In a large bowl, mix together thoroughly the gooseberries, elderflowers and 2 oz (50 g) of the sugar. Lightly grease a 1½ pt (900 ml) ovenproof dish and arrange the gooseberry mixture in the base. Mix together the oats, breadcrumbs and remaining sugar in a bowl, then rub in the butter. Arrange this mixture evenly on top of the fruit mixture in the dish and bake in the oven for 30–40 minutes until the top is crisp and golden and the gooseberries are soft.

BAKED CHOCOLATE PUDDING
Serves 4–5

3 oz (75 g) margarine, cut into small pieces
3 oz (75 g) caster sugar
3 eggs, separated
3 oz (75 g) self-raising flour
1 oz (25 g) cocoa
½ pt (300 ml) milk
caster sugar

Preheat the oven to 375°F/190°C/Gas Mk 5. Cream the margarine and sugar until soft. Gradually beat in the egg yolks and fold in the flour and cocoa. Gradually pour in the milk, beating constantly. Beat the egg whites until they form stiff peaks and fold in. Put the mixture in a lightly greased shallow casserole dish and stand in a tin of water. Bake in the oven for 45 minutes until the pudding has a moist texture underneath with a light fluffy texture on top. Sprinkle with caster sugar and serve hot or cold.

BISCUITS AND CAKES

KIWI BISCUITS
Makes 30

2 oz (50 g) golden syrup
5 oz (150 g) butter
4 oz (110 g) caster sugar
3 oz (75 g) rolled oats
2 oz (50 g) desiccated coconut
4 oz (110 g) plain flour
2 tsp bicarbonate of soda

Preheat the oven to 325°F/170°C/Gas Mk 3. Melt the syrup, butter and sugar in a saucepan over low heat. Remove from the heat and stir in the oats, coconut and flour. Dissolve the bicarbonate of soda in 1 tbsp of hot water and stir into the biscuit mixture, blending well. Leave aside to cool for a few minutes. Divide the mixture into 30 pieces, roll into balls and arrange on greased baking trays, leaving plenty of room between them. Bake in the oven for 20 minutes until browned. Remove from the oven and leave to firm up on the baking trays. Transfer to a wire rack to cool.

SWISS ROLL
Makes 6 slices

3 eggs
3 oz (75 g) caster sugar
1 tbsp boiling water
3 oz (75 g) self-raising flour, sifted
6 tbsp jam

Preheat the oven to 400°F/200°C/Gas Mk 6. Grease a Swiss roll tin and line with greased greaseproof paper, leaving 1 inch (2.5 cm) above the rim of the tin. Whisk the eggs and sugar together until very thick – the whisk should leave a trail when it is lifted. Carefully fold in the sifted flour with the boiling water. Pour into the tin, making sure that the mixture spreads into the corners. Bake in the oven for about 10 minutes or until springy to the touch. Dust a large piece of greaseproof paper with caster sugar and set on a damp tea towel. Turn the cake out onto the sugar and trim the edges with a sharp knife. Spread with jam, roll up from the shortest edge and leave to cool.

ICED RAISIN COOKIES
Makes 25

4 oz (110 g) butter
6 oz (175 g) soft brown sugar
1 egg, beaten
8 oz (225 g) plain flour
2 tsp baking powder
1 tsp each ground cinnamon and mixed spice
pinch salt
4 tbsp soured cream
2 tbsp milk
4 oz (110 g) raisins
4 oz (110 g) icing sugar
¼ tsp vanilla essence

Preheat the oven to 350°F/180°C/Gas Mk 4. Cream the butter and brown sugar together until light and fluffy. Add the egg a little at a time, beating well after each addition. Sift together the flour, baking powder, cinnamon, mixed spice and salt, then fold into the creamed mixture alternately with the soured cream, milk and raisins. Drop tablespoonfuls onto a greased baking sheet, leaving plenty of space in between for them to spread. Bake in the oven for about 15 minutes or until brown. Remove the baking sheet from the oven. Sift the icing sugar into a bowl and stir in 3 tbsp boiling water and the vanilla essence. Brush this over the cookies and return to the oven for 5 minutes. Remove from the oven and leave to cool on a wire rack.

MELTING MOMENTS
Makes 12

4 oz (110 g) margarine, cut into small pieces
3 oz (75 g) sugar
½ tsp vanilla essence
1 egg yolk
5 oz (150 g) self-raising flour, sifted
crushed cornflakes

Preheat the oven to 375°F/190°C/Gas Mk 5. Cream the margarine and sugar well. Beat in the vanilla essence and egg yolk. Add the flour and mix to a smooth dough. With wet hands, form the dough into small balls and roll them in the cornflakes. Arrange on greased baking sheets and bake in the oven for 15–20 minutes. Transfer to wire racks to cool.

MOCHA COOKIES
Makes 10

8 oz (225 g) butter, cut into small pieces
4 oz (110 g) caster sugar
8 oz (225 g) self-raising flour
2 oz (50 g) cocoa powder
Filling:
2 oz (50 g) cocoa powder
¼ pt (150 ml) strong coffee
2 oz (50 g) butter
sugar

Preheat the oven to 350°F/180°C/Gas Mk 4. Cream the butter and sugar together in a bowl, then mix in the flour and cocoa powder. Using lightly floured hands, form the mixture into walnut-sized balls and arrange on greased baking trays. Gently press down the top of each ball. Bake in the oven for 12 minutes. Carefully transfer to wire racks to cool. To make the filling, put the coffee and cocoa in a saucepan and heat until the mixture is thick and creamy. Remove from the heat and beat in the butter, adding sugar to taste. Set aside to cool and use this mixture to sandwich the biscuits together.

FRUITY OAT BISCUITS
Makes 36

6 oz (175 g) margarine, cut into small pieces
6 oz (175 g) sugar
2 eggs, beaten
¼ tsp ground ginger
¼ tsp mixed spice
¼ tsp ground cloves
pinch salt
4 oz (110 g) chopped nuts
4 oz (110 g) sultanas or raisins
6 oz (175 g) rolled oats
4 tbsp milk

Preheat the oven to 375°F/190°C/Gas Mk 5. Beat together the margarine and sugar until light and fluffy. Add the remaining ingredients with enough milk to form a smooth, stiff consistency. Drop teaspoonfuls of the mixture onto a greased baking sheet about 2 inches (5 cm) apart. Bake in the oven for 10 minutes or until the biscuits are light golden brown.

CHOCOLATE CRACKLES
Makes 12

8 oz (225 g) chocolate dots
1 oz (25 g) golden syrup
2 oz (50 g) butter
2 oz (50 g) cornflakes

Put the chocolate dots, syrup and butter in a small bowl. Place the bowl over a saucepan of simmering water and heat until the ingredients have melted and are well blended. Remove from the heat and fold in the cornflakes, mixing well. Place a spoonful of the mixture into 12 paper cases and leave to set.

HAZELNUT SQUARES
Makes 16

2 lb (900 g) demerara sugar
½ pt (300 ml) water
1 tsp vanilla essence
3 oz (75 g) chopped hazelnuts

Put the sugar and water in a heavy-based saucepan and heat quickly until the sugar has dissolved. Boil until a drop of the mixture placed in cold water forms a soft ball when rolled between the fingers. Stir in the vanilla essence and nuts and continue boiling for a few minutes. Remove from the heat, leave to cool a little, then beat well. Pour into a greased shallow square tin and leave to cool. When nearly set, cut into pieces.

GINGER SHORTBREAD
Makes 16–20

8 oz (225 g) butter, cut into small pieces
9 oz (250 g) light brown sugar
1 lb (450 g) plain flour, sifted
4 tsp ground ginger
3 oz (75 g) chopped mixed peel

Preheat the oven to 300°F/150°C/Gas Mk 2. Cream together the butter and sugar. Add the flour, ginger and peel and mix thoroughly. Put the mixture into a greased large Swiss roll tin and bake in the oven for 30 minutes. Leave in the tin to cool, then cut into squares.

FLAPJACKS
Makes 12

4 oz (110 g) margarine
4 tbsp golden syrup
3 oz (75 g) granulated sugar
8 oz (225 g) rolled oats
¼ tsp salt

Preheat the oven to 325°F/170°C/Gas Mk 3. Put the margarine and syrup in a saucepan and heat gently until the margarine has melted. Remove from the heat and stir in the sugar, oats and salt. Mix until well blended. Pour the mixture into a greased square shallow tin and cook in the oven for 30–40 minutes until golden brown. Leave to cool in the tin for about 5 minutes, then cut into 12 bars. Transfer to a wire rack to cool.

CHERRY AND DATE FRUIT CAKE
Serves 8

8 oz (225 g) margarine
6 oz (175 g) caster sugar
3 large eggs
¼ tsp vanilla essence
12 oz (350 g) plain flour, sifted
2 tsp baking powder
¼ tsp mixed spice
pinch salt
4 oz (110 g) chopped mixed peel
4 oz (110 g) glacé cherries, halved, rinsed and dried
4 oz (110 g) dried dates, chopped
¼ pt (150 ml) cold tea

Preheat the oven to 325°F/170°C/Gas Mk 3. Grease a 7 inch (17.5 cm) square cake tin and line with greased greaseproof paper. Put the margarine and sugar in a bowl and cream until light and fluffy. Gradually add the eggs, beating well, then the vanilla essence. In another bowl, mix together the flour, baking powder, mixed spice and salt. Gradually fold the flour mixture and the peel, cherries and dates alternately into the margarine and sugar mixture and then gradually pour in the tea. The mixture should be fairly moist. Transfer to the prepared cake tin, levelling the top and making a slight hollow in the centre of the cake. Bake for about 2 hours until a skewer inserted in the middle of the cake comes out clean. Leave to cool in the tin before removing the greaseproof paper.

ORANGE BARS
Makes 12

6 oz (175 g) plain flour, sifted
2 oz (50 g) semolina
3 oz (75 g) caster sugar
6 oz (175 g) butter
finely grated rind of 1 orange
6 oz (175 g) icing sugar
orange juice

Preheat the oven to 325°F/170°C/Gas Mk 3. Put the flour, semolina and caster sugar in a bowl and mix well. Rub in the butter, then mix in the orange rind. Place in a greased 7 inch (17.5 cm) shallow square tin and press down, levelling the top. Bake in the oven for 45 minutes until firm. To make the topping, mix the icing sugar with enough orange juice to form a thick coating consistency. Spread over the hot biscuits and cook in the oven for 10 minutes. Leave to cool in the tin for 10 minutes, then cut into 12 bar shapes and carefully transfer to wire racks to cool.

CHERRY OAT BISCUITS
Makes 12

3 oz (75 g) plain flour
¼ tsp bicarbonate of soda
2 oz (50 g) glacé cherries, chopped
3 oz (75 g) caster sugar
3 oz (75 g) rolled oats
4 oz (110 g) butter
1 tbsp golden syrup
1 tbsp milk

Preheat the oven to 300°F/150°C/Gas Mk 2. Sift the flour and bicarbonate of soda into a bowl. Add the cherries, sugar and rolled oats and mix thoroughly. Put the butter and syrup in a small saucepan and heat until the butter has melted. Pour in the milk stirring well, then remove from the heat and mix into the flour mixture. Mix well until thoroughly blended. Chill in the refrigerator for about 5 minutes. Make small balls of the dough and arrange on lightly greased baking sheets leaving room for the biscuits to spread. Press down the top and bake in the oven for 20–25 minutes until golden brown. Leave to cool on baking sheets for a few minutes, then transfer to wire racks.

LEMON AND ALMOND CAKE
Serves 8

6 oz (175 g) margarine
6 oz (175 g) caster sugar
3 eggs, beaten
2 oz (50 g) lemon curd
finely grated rind of ½ large lemon
few drops almond essence
2 oz (50 g) ground almonds
6 oz (175 g) self-raising flour, sifted
1 oz (25 g) flaked almonds

Preheat the oven to 325°F/170°C/Gas Mk 3. Grease an 8 inch (20 cm) round cake tin and line with greased greaseproof paper. Cream the margarine and sugar in a bowl until soft. Gradually beat in the eggs, followed by the lemon curd, lemon rind and almond essence to taste. Fold in the flour and ground almonds and mix well until thoroughly blended. Transfer to the prepared cake tin, levelling the top and then sprinkle over the flaked almonds. Bake in the oven for 1–1½ hours until a skewer inserted in the middle of the cake comes out clean. Leave to cool in the tin for 5 minutes before turning out onto a wire rack and removing the greaseproof paper.

SAFFRON ROCK CAKES
Makes 12

1 packet saffron strands, soaked overnight in 4 tbsp hot water
1 egg, beaten
8 oz (225 g) self-raising flour, sifted
pinch salt
3 oz (75 g) butter
3 oz (75 g) granulated sugar
3 oz (75 g) sultanas
1 oz (25 g) chopped mixed peel

Preheat the oven to 375°F/190°C/Gas Mk 5. Grease a baking sheet. Drain the saffron into the beaten egg. Sift the flour and salt together in a bowl and rub in the butter until the mixture resembles fine breadcrumbs. Stir in the sugar, sultanas and peel and mix with the egg mixture. Divide into 12 rough heaps on the baking sheet and bake in the oven on the shelf above the centre for about 20 minutes until firm to the touch and golden brown. Cool on a wire rack.

SESAME SEED CAKE
Serves 8

8 oz (225 g) margarine
13 oz (375 g) caster sugar
5 eggs, beaten
1 tsp vanilla essence
8 oz (225 g) plain flour, sifted
pinch salt
3 tbsp sesame seeds

Preheat the oven to 325°F/170°C/Gas Mk 3. Lightly grease and flour an 8 inch (20 cm) round cake tin. Cream the margarine and sugar in a bowl until fluffy. Gradually beat in the eggs, adding 2 tbsp of flour with the last egg. Mix in the vanilla essence, flour and salt and 2 tbsp of the sesame seeds. Mix thoroughly until well blended. Transfer the mixture to the prepared cake tin and level the surface. Sprinkle the remaining sesame seeds on top. Bake in the oven for 1½–2 hours until a skewer inserted in the middle of the cake comes out clean. Turn out onto a wire tray to cool.

CHOCOLATE CAKE
Serves 8

2 oz (50 g) cocoa powder
8 fl oz (225 ml) boiling water
4 oz (110 g) soft margarine
8 oz (225 g) granulated sugar
2 eggs
7 oz (200 g) plain flour, sifted
1 tsp bicarbonate of soda
¼ tsp baking powder

Preheat the oven to 350°F/180°C/Gas Mk 4. Sift the cocoa powder into a bowl and slowly pour on the boiling water, stirring until smooth. Leave to cool. Beat together the margarine and sugar until light and fluffy, then gradually beat in the eggs. Sift the flour, bicarbonate of soda and baking powder together and fold into the creamed mixture alternately with the cocoa mixture. Pour into a greased, base-lined deep 6½ inch (16 cm) tin and bake for about 45 minutes or until a skewer inserted in the middle of the cake comes out clean. Turn out onto a wire rack and leave to cool.

SHELL CAKES
Makes 12–14

3 oz (75 g) butter
3 oz (75 g) caster sugar
1 small egg, beaten
5 oz (150 g) plain flour, sifted
jam for filling
icing sugar for dredging

Preheat the oven to 400°F/200°C/Gas Mk 6. Put the butter and sugar in a bowl and cream together until light and fluffy. Beat in the egg, fold in the flour and mix well. Put the mixture in a piping bag fitted with a large star nozzle and pipe 12–14 small shapes onto greased baking sheets. Bake in the oven for 10–15 minutes until faintly coloured. Transfer to wire racks to cool. Sandwich together in pairs with the jam and dust the top with icing sugar.

EXOTIC FRUIT ROCK CAKES
Makes 12

12 oz (350 g) plain flour, sifted
3 tsp baking powder
1 tsp mixed spice
6 oz (175 g) butter
2 oz (50 g) desiccated coconut
3 oz (75 g) dried pineapple pieces
3 oz (75 g) dried papaya pieces
3 oz (75 g) demerara sugar
2 eggs, beaten
3 tbsp milk

Preheat the oven to 400°F/200°C/Gas Mk 6. Lightly grease 2 baking sheets. Sift the flour, baking powder and mixed spice into a large bowl and rub in the butter until the mixture resembles fine breadcrumbs. Stir in the coconut, dried pineapple and papaya and sugar and make a well in the centre. Beat the eggs and milk together and pour into the centre of the mix, binding lightly with a fork until a stiff, crumbly mixture is obtained. Place 6 rough heaps of the mixture on each of the greased baking sheets and bake in the oven for about 20 minutes, or until golden brown. Cool on a wire rack.

CINNAMON CAKE
Serves 8–10

4 oz (110 g) butter
2 oz (50 g) soft brown sugar
2 oz (50 g) black treacle
6 oz (175 g) golden syrup
9 oz (250 g) plain flour, sifted
2 tbsp ground cinnamon
1 tsp bicarbonate of soda
¼ pt (150 ml) milk
2 eggs

Preheat the oven to 325°F/170°C/Gas Mk 3. Grease a 9 inch (23 cm) square cake tin and then line it with greased greaseproof paper. Heat the butter, sugar, treacle and golden syrup gently in a pan, stirring until the sugar has dissolved. Sift the flour, cinnamon and bicarbonate of soda into a large bowl and make a well in the centre. Pour in the syrup mixture and stir well, adding the milk a little at a time until a smooth batter is obtained. Lightly whisk the eggs and stir in, then spoon the mixture into the prepared tin. Bake in the oven, on the shelf above the centre, for 50–60 minutes or until cooked through and springy when touched with the fingertips. Cool for 5 minutes in the tin before turning out onto a wire rack to cool completely. Store in an airtight container for at least 24 hours before cutting.

BRACK BREAD
Serves 8

8 oz (225 g) raisins
8 oz (225 g) sultanas
¼ pt (150 ml) hot tea
8 oz (225 g) soft dark brown sugar
8 oz (225 g) wholemeal flour
2 tsp ground mixed spice
2 eggs, beaten

Put the raisins and sultanas in a bowl and pour over the hot tea. Leave to soak for at least 1 hour. Preheat the oven to 350°F/180°C/ Gas Mk 4. Stir in the sugar, flour, mixed spice and eggs and mix well together. Grease and base-line a 2 lb (900 g) loaf tin and spoon in the mixture. Level the top and bake in the centre of the oven for 1 hour or until a skewer inserted in the bread comes out cleanly. Turn out and leave to cool on a wire rack. Serve cold, sliced and buttered.

PLAIN FRUIT CAKE
Serves 8

5 oz (150 g) soft margarine
5 oz (150 g) caster sugar
2 eggs
10 oz (300 g) mixed dried fruit
8 oz (225 g) self-raising flour
1 tsp mixed spice
4 fl oz (125 ml) milk

Preheat the oven to 300°F/150°C/Gas Mk 2. Put all the ingredients in a bowl and mix thoroughly to a soft dropping consistency. Put the mixture into a 7 inch (17.5 cm) lightly oiled round cake tin which has been lined with greased greaseproof paper. Bake in the oven for 2 hours until firm. Transfer to a wire rack to cool.

SHORTBREAD FINGERS
Makes 12

5 oz (150 g) plain flour, sifted
1 oz (25 g) rice flour
2 oz (50 g) caster sugar
4 oz (110 g) butter, cut into small pieces

Preheat the oven to 325°F/170°C/Gas Mk 3. Mix together the flours and sugar in a bowl, add the butter and knead well until the mixture binds together. Put in a greased 7 inch (17.5 cm) square sandwich tin, pressing down and levelling the top. Prick the top a few times with a fork. Bake for 40–45 minutes until golden brown. Using a knife, lightly mark out the top into 12 finger shapes and leave to cool in the tin for about 5 minutes. Cut into the fingers and cool on a wire rack.

BANANA ROCK CAKES
Makes 10

7 oz (200) plain wholemeal flour
1½ tsp baking powder
3 oz (75 g) butter
1 tbsp light brown soft sugar
2 oz (50 g) sultanas
8 oz (225 g) bananas
1 tsp lemon juice
1 egg

Preheat the oven to 400°F/200°C/Gas Mk 6. Sift the flour and baking powder into a bowl. Rub in the butter until the mixture resembles fine breadcrumbs. Stir in the sugar and sultanas. Mash the bananas in a bowl then add the lemon juice. Beat in the egg. Pour into the flour mixture and beat well. Place about ten spoonfuls of the mixture on a baking sheet, arranged to allow room for spreading. Bake for 15 minutes until risen and golden brown. Cool on a wire rack.

SWISS TARTS
Makes 12

8 oz (225 g) butter
2 oz (50 g) caster sugar
vanilla essence
8 oz (225 g) plain flour, sifted
icing sugar for dusting
2 tbsp redcurrant jelly

Preheat the oven to 350°F/180°C/Gas Mk 4. Cream together the butter and sugar in a bowl. Stir in a few drops of vanilla essence then gradually stir in the flour. Place the mixture in a piping bag fitted with a large star nozzle. Place 12 paper cake cases on a baking sheet and pipe in the mixture using a spiral motion. Leave a small hole in the centre. Bake in the oven for 25–30 minutes until golden brown. Leave to cool, then sprinkle icing sugar on top. Place a little redcurrant jelly in the centre of each cake.

COCONUT KISSES
Makes 10

3 oz (75 g) margarine
2 oz (50 g) sugar
4 oz (110 g) self-raising flour, sifted
a little milk
jam
desiccated coconut

Preheat the oven to 400°F/200°C/Gas Mk 6. Cream the butter and sugar together in a bowl. Add the flour and sufficient milk to make a firm dough. Form the dough into marble-sized balls, and put on an ungreased baking sheet. Bake in the oven for 10 minutes. Cool on the baking sheet. When completely cold, use the jam to sandwich together pairs of the biscuits. Brush all over with more jam and roll in the desiccated coconut.

HALF POUND CAKE
Serves 8

8 oz (225 g) butter
8 oz (225 g) caster sugar
4 eggs, beaten
8 oz (225 g) plain white flour, sifted
8 oz (225 g) seedless raisins
8 oz (225 g) mixed currants and sultanas
4 oz (110 g) glacé cherries, halved, rinsed and dried
pinch salt
¼ tsp ground mixed spice
1 tbsp brandy
walnut halves to decorate

Preheat the oven to 300°F/150°C/Gas Mk 2. Cream together the butter and sugar until fluffy. Gradually beat in the eggs. Fold in the flour, fruit, salt and spice and add enough brandy to bring the mixture to a soft dropping consistency. Grease a deep 8 inch (20 cm) round cake tin and line with greaseproof paper. Pile in the cake mixture, level the top and decorate with walnut halves. Bake in the oven for 2–2½ hours. Leave in the cake tin for 30 minutes before transferring to a wire rack to cool.

CHERRY AND ALMOND CAKE
Serves 6–8

8 oz (225 g) wholemeal flour
4 oz (110 g) soft light brown sugar
4 oz (110 g) soft margarine
4 oz (110 g) chopped glacé cherries
few drops almond essence
1 egg, beaten
5 tbsp milk
2 tbsp flaked almonds

Preheat the oven to 350°F/180°C/Gas Mk 4. Put the flour and sugar in a bowl and rub in the margarine. Sift the chopped cherries in a little extra flour and stir into the mixture with the almond essence. Mix well with the egg and milk. Grease and base-line a 1 lb (450 g) loaf tin and spoon in the mixture, levelling the top and sprinkling with the flaked almonds. Bake in the oven for about 45 minutes or until a skewer inserted into the centre of the cake comes out clean. Turn out onto a wire tray and cool before cutting.

SPICY GINGER CAKE
Serves 12

8 oz (225 g) plain flour, sifted
1 tsp ground ginger
6 oz (175 g) unsalted butter
6 oz (175 g) caster sugar
2 oz (50 g) crystallised ginger, chopped
1 egg, beaten

Preheat the oven to 350°F/180°C/Gas Mk 4. Grease and base-line an 8 inch (20 cm) sandwich tin. Sift the flour with the ground ginger and rub in the butter. Stir in the chopped ginger and sugar and bind with most of the egg. Knead until pliable and turn into the prepared tin. Level the top and pinch round the edges to decorate. Mark the top in a lattice fashion with a knife and brush with the remaining egg. Bake in the oven for 35–40 minutes until firm to the touch. Cool in the tin.

LEMON CAKE
Serves 6–8

4 oz (110 g) caster sugar
4 oz (110 g) soft margarine
8 oz (225 g) self-raising flour, sifted
grated rind and juice of 1 lemon
2 tbsp milk
1 egg

Topping:
juice of ½ large lemon
2 tbsp caster sugar

Preheat the oven to 350°F/180°C/Gas Mk 4. Cream the sugar and margarine well, then add the flour, lemon rind and juice, milk and egg and beat well. Grease and base-line a deep 7 inch (17.5 cm) tin and spoon in the mixture, levelling the top. Bake for 45 minutes or a skewer inserted in the centre of the cake comes out clean. To make the topping, melt the 2 tbsp caster sugar in the lemon juice, prick the top of the cake with a fork or skewer and pour over the juice and sugar while the cake is still in the tin. Leave to cool and then turn out.

SWEETS

PEPPERMINT ICE
Makes 20–30

1 lb (450 g) granulated sugar
¼ pt (150 ml) milk
1 tsp peppermint essence
few drops green food colouring

Put the sugar and milk in a heavy-based saucepan and stir well. Bring to the boil and continue to boil, stirring occasionally, until a drop of the mixture placed in cold water forms a small ball hard enough to retain its shape. Remove from the heat, add the peppermint essence and stir until the mixture becomes thick. Add the green food colouring. Dampen the inside of a shallow square tin and pour in the mixture. Leave to cool, then cut into pieces.

MARSHMALLOW
Makes 36

10 oz (300 g) granulated sugar
2 tsp powdered glucose
¾ oz (15 g) gelatine
½ pt (300 ml) tepid water
1–2 tbsp orange flower water
1 egg white, stiffly beaten
icing sugar

Put the sugar and glucose in a heavy-based saucepan together with ¼ pt (150 ml) of the tepid water and heat until the sugar has dissolved. Boil until a small drop of the mixture placed in cold water forms a small ball which is hard enough to retain its shape. In the meantime, dissolve the gelatine in the remaining tepid water in a bowl. Keep warm. Whisk the gelatine into the boiling sugar and water. Add the orange flower water, followed by the egg white, whisking all the time. The mixture should reach a thick and stiff consistency, which may take as long as 20 minutes. Line a shallow square tin with greaseproof paper and sprinkle over the icing sugar. Pour in the marshmallow mixture and leave to set. Cut into small rounds or squares, roll in icing sugar and leave to dry for about a day.

MACAROONS
Makes 16

2 large egg whites
4 oz (110 g) ground almonds
6 oz (175 g) caster sugar
1 oz (25 g) ground rice
few drops almond essence
8 blanched almonds

Preheat the oven to 300°F/150°C/Gas Mk 2. Line two large baking trays with rice paper. Place 1 tsp of the egg white in a bowl and set aside. Place the remaining egg white in a bowl and whisk until it forms soft peaks. Fold in the almonds, sugar, ground rice and almond essence to taste and mix thoroughly. Arrange about 16 heaped teaspoons of the mixture on the rice paper, pressing down the top slightly. Place half an almond on top of each one and brush with the reserved egg white. Bake for 25–30 minutes until golden brown. Leave to cool slightly in the baking tray before cutting away the excess rice paper from around each macaroon. When the cakes are completely cold, store in an airtight tin.

FRUIT AND NUT FUDGE
Makes 20

2 lb (900 g) sugar
½ pt (300 ml) milk
4 oz (110 g) margarine
½ tsp vanilla essence
2 oz (50 g) sultanas
2 oz (50 g) walnuts, chopped

Put the sugar and milk in a saucepan and leave to soak for 1 hour, then cook gently over low heat until the sugar has dissolved. Drop in the margarine and when this has melted, bring the mixture to the boil. Cook until a little of the mixture dropped in cold water forms a soft ball. Remove from the heat, leave to cool slightly, then beat well until the fudge is creamy and thick. Stir in the vanilla essence, sultanas and walnuts and quickly pour into a well-greased shallow Swiss roll tin. Smooth the top and mark out into small squares. Leave to cool and set, then cut into the squares.

ROSEHIP CREAMS
Makes 18

5 tsp lemon juice
½ tsp finely grated lemon rind
4 tsp rosehip syrup
few drops vanilla essence
8 oz (225 g) icing sugar, sifted
½ oz (10 g) crystallised rose petals

Put the lemon juice and rind, rosehip syrup and vanilla essence in a bowl. Stir in the icing sugar and mix to a smooth paste-like consistency. Divide into about 18 pieces and shape into balls. Arrange on a flat dish covered with icing sugar and press a rose petal in the centre of each one. Leave to dry in a cool place.

TURKISH DELIGHT
Makes 45

½ pt (300 ml) hot water
1 oz (25 g) gelatine
1 lb (450 g) granulated sugar
¼ tsp citric acid
few drops vanilla essence
few drops almond essence
red food colouring
2 oz (50 g) icing sugar
1 oz (25 g) cornflour

Pour the water into a heavy-based saucepan. Sprinkle in the gelatine, add the sugar and citric acid and heat gently until the sugar has dissolved. Boil for 20 minutes. Remove from the heat and set aside for 10 minutes to cool. Stir in a few drops of vanilla and almond essence. Pour half the mixture into a shallow square tin. Stir a few drops of food colouring into the remaining mixture and then pour this in the tin. Leave to cool for 1 day. Lay out a sheet of greaseproof paper. Mix together the icing sugar and cornflour and sprinkle some on the paper. Turn out the mixture from the tin onto the paper. Cut into squares and roll in the remaining icing sugar and cornflour mixture. Wrap the Turkish delight in greaseproof paper before storing in an airtight tin.

FRESH FRUIT JELLIES
Makes 36

¼ pt (150 ml) fruit juice
3 oz (75 g) granulated sugar
6 tbsp powdered glucose
1 oz (25 g) gelatine
caster sugar

Heat the fruit juice and sugar gently in a small saucepan over low heat until the sugar has dissolved. Stir in the glucose and gelatine until the gelatine has dissolved. Dampen a 6 inch (15 cm) square tin, pour in the mixture and leave to set. Dip the tin in hot water for a few seconds, then turn out the jelly onto a flat surface. Cut into small squares and roll in caster sugar.

PEANUT BRITTLE
Makes 24 bars

12 oz (350 g) unsalted peanuts, chopped
14 oz (400 g) granulated sugar
6 oz (175 g) light soft brown sugar
6 oz (175 g) golden syrup
¼ pt (150 ml) water
2 oz (50 g) butter
¼ tsp bicarbonate of soda

Put the nuts on a baking sheet and warm in the oven for a few minutes. Put the sugars, syrup and water in a large, heavy-based saucepan and heat until the sugars dissolve. Add the butter, bring to the boil and cook until a little of the mixture dropped in cold water separates into threads and becomes hard and brittle. Lower the heat, and add the bicarbonate of soda and warmed nuts. Pour the mixture slowly into a buttered 12 x 4 inch (30 x 10 cm) shallow tin and, when almost set, mark into bars.

CREAM CARAMELS
Makes 20

8 oz (225 g) light soft brown sugar
2 tbsp water
4 oz (110 g) butter
few drops vanilla essence
3 tbsp single cream

Heat the sugar and water in a heavy-based saucepan until the sugar
has dissolved. Stir in the butter, vanilla essence and cream and boil
until a drop of the mixture dropped in cold water forms a ball which
retains its shape. Pour the mixture into an oiled 6 inch (15 cm) square
tin and leave to cool. When almost cold, mark into squares. When
firmly set, cut out the squares and wrap in waxed paper.

CREAMY TOFFEE
Makes 35–45

1 lb (450 g) light soft brown sugar
6 tbsp milk
1 tbsp golden syrup
2 oz (50 g) butter
1 small can condensed milk

Heat the sugar and milk in a heavy-based saucepan until the sugar
dissolves. Add the syrup and butter and bring to the boil. Continue to
boil for 2–3 minutes and then stir in the condensed milk. Bring back
to the boil and continue boiling until a drop of the mixture placed in
cold water forms a soft ball when rolled in the fingers. Remove from
the heat, beat until thick and creamy and pour into a buttered shallow
square tin. Mark into squares, leave to set, then cut into the squares.

CHOCOLATE RAISIN FUDGE
Makes 35

2 tbsp seedless raisins
2 tbsp sherry
4 oz (110 g) plain chocolate
2 oz (50 g) butter
4 tbsp evaporated milk
12 oz (350 g) icing sugar

Put the raisins in a dish, pour over the sherry and leave to soak overnight. Put the chocolate and butter in a small bowl placed over a saucepan of simmering water and stir until melted. Remove from the heat and stir in the evaporated milk and drained raisins. Gradually stir the icing sugar into the mixture until smooth and thick. Grease a shallow tin with butter and line with waxed paper. Press the fudge into the tin and leave to cool. When cold, cut into squares.

CHERRY TRUFFLES
Makes 12–16

4 oz (110 g) fine cake crumbs
grated rind of 1 small orange
1 oz (25 g) glacé cherries, finely chopped
2 oz (50 g) caster sugar
1 oz (25 g) ground almonds
4 tbsp apricot jam
1 tsp water
chocolate vermicelli

Mix together the cake crumbs, orange rind, cherries, sugar and almonds in a bowl. Heat the jam and water in a small saucepan, then sieve into the cake crumb mixture. Mix until well blended. Form into small balls and place on waxed paper. Roll in the vermicelli, leave to dry and then place in paper cases.

CHOCOLATE CREAM TRUFFLES
Makes 12

4½ oz (120 g) plain chocolate
4 tbsp double cream
2 tsp angostura bitters
3 oz (75 g) cocoa powder
4 oz (110 g) icing sugar

Break the chocolate into small pieces and put in a small bowl placed over a saucepan of simmering water. When the chocolate has melted, remove from the heat and leave to cool slightly. Whisk the cream until stiff. Fold the chocolate and bitters into the cream and leave until cold. Mix the icing sugar and 2 oz (50 g) of the cocoa powder together in a bowl, then beat into the chocolate mixture. Shape into small balls and toss in the remaining cocoa powder.

LOLLIPOPS
Makes 10

8 oz (225 g) granulated sugar
4 oz (110 g) golden syrup
¼ pt (150 ml) water
lollipop sticks

Heat the sugar, syrup and water gently in a heavy-based saucepan until the sugar dissolves. Bring to the boil and cook until a small drop of the mixture placed in cold water forms a ball firm enough to retain its shape. Oil an enamel flat surface and pour on spoonfuls of the mixture so it forms rounds. Place a lollipop stick into each round while soft, then pour over more mixture to cover the stick. Leave to set, then lift off from the work surface and wrap in cellophane.

COCONUT ICE BARS
Makes 10

1 lb (450 g) granulated sugar
¼ pt (150 ml) milk
5 oz (150 g) desiccated coconut
few drops red food colouring (optional)

Put the sugar and milk in a heavy-based saucepan and cook over low heat until the sugar dissolves. Boil gently for 10 minutes. Remove from the heat and gradually stir in the coconut. Pour half the mixture into a buttered 8 x 6 inch (20 x 15 cm) shallow tin. Add a few drops of the red food colouring to the remaining half of the liquid then pour this into the tin. Leave aside until half set, mark out into small bars and cut out the bars when the mixture is thoroughly set.

TOFFEE APPLES
Makes 6–8

1 lb (450 g) demerara sugar
2 oz (50 g) butter
2 tsp vinegar
¼ pt (150 ml) water
1 tbsp golden syrup
6–8 medium apples
6–8 wooden sticks

Gently heat the sugar, butter, vinegar, water and syrup in a heavy-based saucepan until the sugar has dissolved and the butter has melted. Boil rapidly for 5 minutes until a drop of the mixture placed in cold water separates into threads which become hard but not brittle. Wash and dry the apples and impale on the sticks. Dip each one into the toffee mixture, swirling it around, so that the excess toffee drips back into the saucepan. Leave to cool on a buttered baking sheet.

CHOCOLATE DATES
Makes 20

1 lb (450 g) dessert dates
4 oz (110 g) plain chocolate, grated
1 tbsp boiling water
½ tsp vanilla essence

Using a sharp knife, cut the dates lengthwise and remove the stones leaving the dates intact. Put the chocolate, vanilla essence and boiling water in a small saucepan and stir well over low heat until the chocolate has melted. Remove and place the saucepan in a larger saucepan full of boiling water so that the chocolate does not harden too quickly. Gently press open the dates, spoon in some melted chocolate and press the sides of the dates back together. Arrange in sweet papers.

BUTTERSCOTCH APPLES
Serves 6

6 dessert apples
4 oz (110 g) butter
4 oz (110 g) soft brown sugar
3 tbsp single cream
vanilla essence

Peel, core and slice the apples and place in a bowl. Place some cling film over the top. Place the butter in a saucepan over low heat until melted. Add the sugar, cream and a few drops of vanilla essence to taste and stir slowly until the sugar dissolves. Boil for 5 minutes. Add the apple slices and cook gently for 7–10 minutes, turning the apple occasionally. Keep warm in a saucepan until ready to serve.

BUTTERSCOTCH
Makes 35

1 lb (450 g) demerara sugar
¼ pt (150 ml) water
2–3 oz (50–75 g) unsalted butter

Put the sugar and water in a heavy-based saucepan and cook over low heat until the sugar has dissolved. Increase the heat and boil until a little of the mixture dropped in cold water separates into threads which are hard but not brittle. Use a brush dipped in cold water to brush down the sides of the saucepan during cooking. Gradually add the butter a little at a time, mixing well. Pour the mixture into a buttered 7 x 5 inch (18 x 12.5 cm) shallow tin. When almost set, cut into squares.

FRENCH TRUFFLES
Makes 12–16

12 oz (350 g) milk chocolate
5 tbsp single cream
½ tsp vanilla essence
chopped nuts of choice

Melt the chocolate in a bowl set over a saucepan of simmering water. Scald the cream and let it stand until lukewarm. Beat the chocolate until smooth, pour in the cream and beat well. Stir in the vanilla essence until well blended. Line a medium tin with waxed paper and pour in the truffle mixture. Leave in a cool place until firm. Form into small balls and then roll these in chopped nuts of your choice.

AMERICAN CANDY
Makes 40

12 oz (350 g) preserving sugar
4–6 tbsp water
6 oz (175 g) seedless raisins, chopped
2 oz (50 g) blanched almonds, chopped

Put the sugar and water in a heavy-based saucepan and heat gently until the mixture becomes a golden brown syrup. Stir in the raisins and almonds and press the mixture into a buttered 7 inch (17.5 cm) shallow tin. When the mixture has nearly set, cut into squares.

DRINKS

BLACKCURRANT FLOAT
Serves 4

1 pt (600 ml) milk
4 tbsp blackcurrant jam, sieved, or ¼ pt (150 ml) fresh blackcurrant purée
sugar to taste
few drops red food colouring
vanilla ice cream

Whisk the milk, jam or purée, sugar and red colouring together in a blender and chill well. Pour into tall glasses and top with a spoonful of vanilla ice cream.

MOCHA CREAMS
Serves 3

1 pt (600 ml) milk
1 tbsp instant coffee granules
1 tbsp cocoa powder
sugar to taste
2 tbsp whipped cream

Gently heat the milk, coffee and cocoa powder in a saucepan. Liquidise until frothy, adding sugar to taste. Pour into large mugs and add a spoonful of whipped cream to serve.

CHOCOLATE CREAM SODA
Serves 1

1 tbsp double cream
3 tbsp chocolate syrup
2 tbsp chocolate ice cream
soda water

Place the cream and syrup in a tall glass and mix thoroughly. Stir in the chocolate ice cream, top up with soda water and stir.

PINEAPPLE COBBLER
Serves 6

1 pt (600 ml) grapefruit juice
juice of ½ lemon
10 oz (300 g) canned pineapple cubes
cucumber peel
sugar to taste
1 pt (600 ml) soda
cocktail cherries
crushed ice

Pour the grapefruit and lemon juices into a jug and mix well. Leave in the refrigerator to chill. Add the pineapple cubes, some cucumber peel and sugar to taste. Stir in the soda. To serve, place a cherry in each glass and pour in the liquid over crushed ice.

GINGERED RAISIN PUNCH
Serves 6

1 tbsp clear honey
2 oz (50 g) raisins
grated rind and juice of 1 lemon
1 pt (600 ml) apple juice
ice cubes
1 pt (600 ml) ginger ale
1 orange, peeled and segmented
1 apple, cored and segmented

In a large wide jug mix together the honey, raisins, lemon rind and juice. Cover and leave for a few hours. Pour in the apple juice and add some ice cubes. Add the ginger ale and float the orange and apple segments on top.

ALMOND MILK
Serves 4

4 oz (110 g) chopped almonds
1¼ pt (750 ml) water
1 tbsp sugar
1 tbsp orange juice

Put the water and almonds in a bowl. Stir well until the liquid becomes milky white. Strain and leave the almonds to dry, then pound them into a powder. Add the almond powder to the milky white liquid, then add the orange juice and sugar. Serve well chilled.

LEMONADE
Serves 2

3 large lemons
8 oz (225 g) sugar
4 fl oz (125 ml) water

To make the lemon syrup, grate the rind of 1 lemon and place in a saucepan together with the sugar and water. Heat gently until the sugar has dissolved, then boil for 5 minutes. Leave to cool, then add the strained juice of 3 lemons. To serve use 1 measure lemon syrup to 2 measures soda or plain water in a glass with ice.

ORANGE FLUFF
Serves 1

2 tbsp undiluted orange squash
¼ pt (150 ml) milk
1 oz (25 g) vanilla ice cream

Whisk together the orange squash, the milk and half the ice cream until frothy. Pour into a long glass and top with the remaining ice cream. Decorate with a thin slice of orange if desired.

PEACH HONEY CREAM
Serves 6

12 oz (350 g) fresh peaches, skinned, stoned and crushed
6 oz (175 g) clear honey
1¾ pt (1 L) milk
½ tsp almond essence
1¾ pt (1 L) vanilla ice cream

Place the peaches and honey in a bowl and mix well. Stir in half the quantity of milk, beat well, then add the remaining milk. Stir in the almond essence and half the quantity of ice cream. Beat thoroughly until smooth. Pour into individual glasses and place a small scoop of the remaining ice cream on top.

RASPBERRY MILKSHAKE
Serves 2

½ pt (300 ml) milk
¼ pt (150 ml) raspberry-flavoured yoghurt
4 oz (110 g) fresh raspberries

Liquidise the milk, yoghurt and most of the raspberries, blending until frothy. Pour into glasses and place the remaining fruit on top to serve.

CHOCOMINT
Serves 1

4 tsp drinking chocolate powder
ice cold milk
few drops peppermint essence
whipped cream
chocolate curls, to decorate

Dissolve the drinking chocolate with just enough boiling water to melt it. Chill. Add the ice cold milk and top with a swirl of whipped cream. Decorate with chocolate curls.

FRUIT YOGHURT SHAKE
Serves 1

¼ pt (150 ml) fruit yoghurt
½ ripe banana
1 tsp clear honey
1 ice cube
1 scoop vanilla ice cream to decorate

Liquidise the yoghurt, banana, and honey, blending well until frothy. Place the ice cube in a glass, pour over the yoghurt mixture and add a scoop of ice cream on the top to serve.

COFFEE FLOATER
Serves 1–2

1 tsp instant coffee granules
1 tsp clear honey
½ pt (300 ml) ice cold milk
coffee or vanilla ice cream

Dissolve the coffee and honey with a little boiling water. Add the ice cold milk and chill. Float a square of ice cream on the top.

LIME SODA
Serves 4

1 small ripe banana
3 tbsp lime cordial
1 pt (600 ml) vanilla ice cream
½ pt (300 ml) soda water
slices of lime, to decorate

Liquidise the banana, lime cordial and half the ice cream, blending until smooth and frothy. Pour into individual glasses and float scoops of the remaining ice cream on top. Hook a lime slice on to the edge of the glass before serving.

SPICED FRUIT PUNCH
Serves 10

1 pt (600 ml) orange juice
½ pt (300 ml) pineapple juice
juice and rind of 1 lemon
½ tsp each ground nutmeg and ground mixed spice
6 cloves
1 pt (600 ml) water
4–6 oz (110–175 g) caster sugar
1¼ pt (750 ml) ginger ale, chilled
crushed ice

Put the fruit juices, spices and lemon rind in a large jug. Put the water and sugar in a saucepan and bring to the boil. When the sugar has dissolved, leave to cool, and then add to the ingredients in the jug. Chill. Just before serving, strain the liquid and add the ginger ale and crushed ice.

GOLDEN PUNCH
Serves 20

1 pt (600 ml) lemon juice, chilled
1 pt (600 ml) orange juice, chilled
1 pt (600 ml) cold water
14 oz (400 g) caster sugar
6 pt (3.4 L) ginger ale, chilled
fresh orange and lemon slices
fresh mint leaves

Combine the fruit juices, sugar and water in a large punch bowl. Stir until the sugar dissolves. Just before serving pour the ginger ale down the side of the bowl and stir gently. Float thin slices of fresh orange and lemon and mint leaves on top.

VEGETABLE AND FRUIT CUP
Serves 4

¼ pt (150 ml) carrot juice
½ pt (300 ml) apple juice
¼ pt (150 ml) orange juice
¼ cucumber, peeled and sliced
6 ice cubes
fresh mint sprigs

Blend together the juices, cucumber and ice cubes in an electric blender until smooth. Pour into individual glasses and float a sprig of mint on top of each glass.

STRAWBERRY CREAM PUNCH
Serves 4–6

14 oz (400 g) can pineapple juice, chilled
1¾ pt (1 L) bottle lemonade, chilled
3 oz (75 g) caster sugar
1½ pt (900 ml) strawberry ice cream
1½ pt (900 ml) ginger ale, chilled
few fresh strawberries

In punch bowl mix the pineapple juice, lemonade and sugar and stir well until the sugar has dissolved. Add the ice cream and stir again until blended. Stir in the ginger ale and float halved strawberries on top to serve.

MELON CRUSH
Serves 4

1 small honeydew melon
¼ tsp ground ginger
¼ pt (150 ml) yoghurt
ice cubes
carbonated mineral water

Peel and deseed the melon. Chop the flesh and place in a liquidiser together with the ginger and yoghurt. Blend until very smooth. Chill in the refrigerator. Before serving add ice cubes and mineral water to taste.

GRAPEFRUIT MINT PUNCH
Serves 12

12 oz (350 g) caster sugar
8 fl oz (225 ml) cold water
1½ pt (900 ml) orange juice, chilled
8 fl oz (225 ml) lemon juice
8 fl oz (225 ml) grapefruit juice
1½ pt (900 ml) soda water, chilled
fresh mint sprigs

Mix together the sugar and water in a saucepan. Bring to the boil and simmer for 3 minutes. Mix together all the remaining ingredients in a bowl and add the melted sugar. Stir well and chill. Float mint sprigs on top to serve.

INDEX